Praise for *The Book of Giving*

"Pierce Hibbs is a friend. He loves the Lord, and he understands well the English language. He is adept in the many ways in which we can communicate the gospel to one another. The present book treats 'giving' as a perspective from which we can view all of Scripture, for Scripture is the story of the greatest gift of all, the Father's gift of the Son to save us from sin and to fill us with his own gifts in the Spirit. The book is filled with great learning aids: Bible references, poetry, charts, reflection questions. Pierce wants us to take Scripture into our hearts and allow it to examine our lives in detail. This is a great devotional guide for believers, families, and couples."

– **John M. Frame**, author of *Systematic Theology* and the Theology of Lordship series

"An absolutely delightful, beautiful, and profound book, written simply and poetically. Receive the gift and rejoice."

– **Vern S. Poythress**, author of *The Mystery of the Trinity* and *In the Beginning Was the Word*

"A passing glance at this book's title, *The Book of Giving*, may suggest, 'Oh, another manual on giving....' But that is what this book most certainly is not! Rather, it is a thoughtful, biblical, and intentionally lyrical call to enter the divine circle of giving because, as the author notes, 'sometimes we need the truth to be lyrical for it to sink into our souls.' And because it is soul-penetrating, it is more practical than the erstwhile manuals because it invites us into the trinitarian orb of giving and the ongoing stewardship of all that we have. The book's practicality is enhanced by the (yes!) lyrical poem-prayers that conclude each section and the recommended exercises to promote growth in giving. Do you want to become a giver after God's heart? Spend time in the remarkable pages of this book."

– **R. Kent Hughes**, Senior Pastor Emeritus of College Church in Wheaton. Former Visiting Professor of Pastoral Theology at Westminster Theological Seminary, Philadelphia

"I have read many books on giving. Even the best of them exhausted me, as they generally *take* more than they give. Enter Pierce Hibbs's *The Book of Giving*. What a gift! As in all his writing, Hibbs captures you with fresh and lively word-craft, illustrative wizardry, and heart-warming metaphor. But the deeper beauty of this book lies not in its artfulness, but in its burden-lifting, life-giving expression of biblical truth. Page after page unwraps profound theological insights, offering soul-nourishing delicacies with grace-filled usefulness. With one jaw-dropping glimpse after another at the practical relevance (yes!) of the Trinity, Hibbs exposes how and why the self-giving

Triune God 'makes us givers by drawing us into his circle.' To read *The Book of Giving* is to get swept into this vivifying circle! But let me warn you. Don't read this book if you'd rather abide in your prison cell of self-interest and clutch your shackles of remorse. *The Book of Giving* may well demolish the chains, and ignite your soul with such a newfound grasp of Trinitarian self-giving, you will soar to new heights of giving and plummet new depths of joy."

 – **Dr. David B. Garner**, Academic Dean and Vice President of Global Ministries, Westminster Theological Seminary

Other Books by the Author

- *The Trinity, Language, and Human Behavior: A Reformed Exposition of the Language Theory of Kenneth L. Pike*
- *In Divine Company: Growing Closer to the God Who Speaks*
- *Theological English: An Advanced ESL Text for Students of Theology*
- *Finding God in the Ordinary*
- *The Speaking Trinity & His Worded World: Why Language Is at the Center of Everything*
- *Struck Down but Not Destroyed: Living Faithfully with Anxiety*
- *Still, Silent, and Strong: Meditations for the Anxious Heart, V. 1*
- *Finding Hope in Hard Things: A Positive Take on Suffering*

To receive free downloads and connect with the author, visit piercetaylorhibbs.com.

Connect and Learn More!

Want access to more resources for growing as a giver? Check out the reader resource page for this book. Go to http://piercetaylorhibbs.com/the-book-of-giving-reader-resources/. You can also follow the author on Twitter (@HibbsPierce), Instagram (@pthibbs), and Facebook (@wordsfromPTH). To download a free ebook from the author, visit http://piercetaylorhibbs.com/subscribe-and-connect/.

THE BOOK OF GIVING

How the God Who Gives Can Make Us Givers

by

PIERCE TAYLOR HIBBS

THE BOOK OF GIVING
How the God Who Gives Can Make Us Givers

Paperback ISBN: 978-1-7363411-2-4
Hardback ISBN: 978-1-7363411-3-1

Cover art by Jessica Hiatt

For Christina, who always gives and so seldom takes.

Contents

Giving is what we do best. It is the air into which we are born. It is the action that was designed into us before our birth. Giving is the way the world is. God gives himself. He also gives away everything that is. He makes no exceptions for any of us. We are given away to our families, to our neighbors, to our friends, to our enemies—to the nations. Our life is for others. That is the way creation works. Some of us try desperately to hold on to ourselves, to live for ourselves. We look so bedraggled and pathetic doing it, hanging on to the dead branch of a bank account for dear life, afraid to risk ourselves on the untried wings of giving. We don't think we can live generously because we have never tried. But the sooner we start the better, for we are going to have to give up our lives finally, and the longer we wait the less time we have for the soaring and swooping life of grace.

— **Eugene Peterson**, *Run with the Horses*

Introduction

"What do you have that you did not receive?" 1 Corinthians 4:7

I sit open-palmed at my desk in the morning dark. I am waiting. Waiting for God to give me words. Does that sound strange to you? It *is* strange—not in some weird cultic sense but in the Christmas sense. What right do I have to come tumbling down the stairs at a thousand gifts? Small gifts. Beautiful gifts. Things I tear open and receive without even a whisper of recognition. These words I write are each wrapped and labeled, ribboned and taped. I did not, do not, and will not ever possess them. They are not my property. They are not yours, either. They are the possessions of a God richer and nobler than a million kings of a million countries.[1]

And yet here we are, you and I, holding them with our eyes, turning over the letters and phrases, lifting them up to the light, tasting them.

You can say the same about your fingers and forearms, your lips and lungs, your chair, your room, the ground beneath you, the oxygen drifting in through your nose and down into your blood stream. We swim in gifts, in things

---

1. I'm committed to Reformed orthodoxy, but in this book I'm exploring the kinds of connections that God invites us to make with the world he's created.

given freely by a God so prodigal that his spending spills well beyond thought.

We swim in gifts, in things given freely by a God so prodigal that his spending spills well beyond thought.

You don't feel this very often though, do you? Neither do I. The greatest irony of being alive is that we treat gifts as possessions, generosity as commonplace, grace as summer grass—something to be stepped on and forgotten with every lifting muscle.

This is a book that assaults that habit. You will need to revisit it again and again (and in a sense, I will need to write it again and again) because we have spiritual amnesia. We habitually forget grace. We unwrap so many gifts every moment that we forget it's Christmas morning, that God is watching every opening, every spark of joy, and every shrug of the shoulders.

He knows we can't thank him every second. And somehow it's okay. Somehow he keeps giving.

But we know also that being ungrateful darkens our lives, that it removes the color from the photo of each day. We *want* to say thank you. And we want to give, too. That's why you're holding this book. This is *The Book of Giving*.

Such a book can only be about God. It's God who gives constantly, prodigally, incessantly. It's in his nature, coursing through his divine Spirit-blood with a golden glow. He gives

- himself to himself;
- himself to us;
- his creation to us;
- us to each other.

God is the grand Giver. All of life, in a sense, is turning us to this truth and conforming us to it. Everything we experience draws us closer to God's *giving circle*, where Giver, Gift, and Recipient dance and exchange, constantly giving, constantly receiving, constantly being a gift.

God gives. Your father dies of cancer and you mourn him. You question. You beg. You pray. But your father was a gift. How will *you* give now? That's the giving circle.

God gives. Your anxiety disorder cripples your body and mind.[2] You question. You beg. You pray again. It's been over twelve years. You've watched the anxiety burn the fat off your soul. And so this, too, was a gift. How will *you* give now? That's the giving circle.

God gives. So this is a book about him. But he's made us to be givers in his shadow, so this is a book about you, too. Take it and keep it as a reminder of who God is and who you are. *We are givers.*

---

2. I've written extensively about this in *Struck Down but Not Destroyed: Living Faithfully with Anxiety* and in *Finding Hope in Hard Things: A Positive Take on Suffering.*

I've ordered the book into three large sections.

- The Triune Giver
- Gifts
- Giving

After laying the groundwork for what a gift is, we'll dive into the first section, backstroking on the expansive beauty of who God is as the triune Giver and who we are as creatures made in his giving image. The second section marvels at the gifts God gives. And the third stares at how we can give in response to God's gifts. But throughout the whole book there is one central idea, a thesis, visited over and over again. It's quite simple, but very profound. **Giving is circular, and God makes us givers by drawing us into his giving circle.**

I should say at the outset that this is a book of water. It should spill into your thoughts and behaviors. To that end, each chapter offers a prayer and reflection questions. Think of them as cups you can use to carry the water of this book wherever you will.

Now, let the giving begin.

Groundwork: What Is a Gift?

What is a gift? Definitions are fuzzier and more mysterious than we often think. That's not to say words don't have clear meanings, only that the meaning given to words is rooted in God.[1] And since God is ultimately mysterious and not able to be controlled, there's a sense in which the meanings of words are mysterious and beyond our full grasp. But I've found it helpful, following the linguist I studied (Kenneth L. Pike), to look at three components to word meanings: (1) what sets the word apart; (2) what variations the word can take on while still retaining its basic meaning; and (3) what contexts the word appears in. Kenneth Pike called this *contrast, variation,* and *distribution.*[2] That sounds a bit technical for most of us, but it's not hard to grasp after you consider an example.

---

1. For more on the nature of language and the mystery of God, see Vern S. Poythress, *In the Beginning Was the Word: Language—A God-Centered Approach* (Wheaton, IL: Crossway, 2009) and Pierce Taylor Hibbs, *The Speaking Trinity & His Worded World: Why Language Is at the Center of Everything* (Eugene, OR: Wipf & Stock, 2018). On the mystery of the Trinity and word meanings, also see Vern S. Poythress, *The Mystery of the Trinity: A Trinitarian Approach to the Attributes of God* (Phillipsburg, NJ: P&R, 2020), 112–116.

2. Kenneth L. Pike, *Linguistic Concepts: An Introduction to Tagmemics* (Lincoln, NE: University of Nebraska Press, 1982).

1. What sets the word apart? We identify something both by what it is and what it isn't. A gift, in our experience, *is* something offered freely, not out of compulsion. It's a benevolent, open-palmed gesture, made in good will, not demanded by another. At the same time, we would say that a gift *isn't* a bribe or a payback. A bribe isn't benevolent; it's deceptive. A payback is demanded by another, and it's not always made in good will.

2. What variations can the word take on while still retaining its basic meaning? A gift can be a package wrapped in paper and ribbons, but it can also be a cup of coffee, a selfless act, and even the eternal salvation of the soul. The language that the Apostle Paul uses for "gift" and "grace" is sometimes identical (especially the Greek word *charis*). The range of what a gift can be runs all the way from a new dress shirt to the person and work of Jesus Christ. Quite a span, isn't it?

3. What contexts does the word appear in? As noted already, a gift can appear in the form of something concrete and tangible, such as an object or money, and also in the form of something abstract—an action in the past or present (Jesus's life, death, and resurrection; the presence and work of the Holy Spirit in our daily lives). But what's critical for us—and we'll keep our eyes on this for the remainder of the book— is that *gifts always occur in the context of relationships.* There's no such thing as a gift that has no giver or recipient. There's always a relationship in which the gift is given. And the gift is meant to do something in that relationship.

The Perfect Gift

What we've noted above aligns in certain ways with what New Testament scholars have learned about the nature of gifts in biblical culture (and how that differs greatly from our twenty-first century Western context). In John Barclay's book *Paul and the Power of Grace*, he delves into a study of what Paul meant by the word *gift*, especially in its relationship to the concept of *grace*, and how this is both familiar and foreign to us today.[3] He lists six ways in which a gift can be "perfected." It's always helpful to look at what the ideal is before talking about specifics, so this is a good place to start. These ways are summarized in the diagram below.

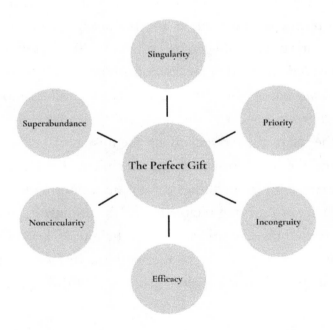

---

3. John M. G. Barclay, *Paul and the Power of Grace* (Grand Rapids, MI: William B. Eerdmans, 2020).

Each facet touches on either the gift, the giver, or the recipient—the triad of any giving act. First, a *superabundant* gift "is perfected in scale, significance, or duration: it is huge, lavish, unceasing, long-lasting, etc."[4] This focuses on the gift itself. Surely, God's gift of salvation in Christ and the gift of the Holy Spirit come to mind. Second, in terms of *singularity*, we focus on the giver. Barclay writes that singularity means that "benevolence or goodness is the giver's *sole* or *exclusive* mode of operation."[5] This is related to what we said about good will and benevolence in our initial discussion of what a gift is. Third is the *priority* of the gift, which deals with time; priority "concerns the timing of the gift, which is given before any initiative taken by the recipient. The prior gift is not a response to a request, and is thus spontaneous in its generosity; it is not obliged by a previous gift."[6] As we noted, a gift isn't demanded or required in any way. Fourth, we have the *incongruity* of the gift, and this is especially important. "Incongruity concerns the relationship between the giver and the recipient, and maximizes the mismatch between the gift and the worth or merit of its recipient. To give lavishly and in advance is one thing, but it is quite another to give to unworthy or unfitting recipients."[7] It's certainly easy to see how something like this applies to the gift of Jesus Christ. None of us was worthy to receive him. In fact, we raged against the gift *as it was given* (Rom. 5:8)! Fifth is the gift's

---

4. Barclay, *Paul and the Power of Grace*, 29, Kindle edition.

5. Barclay, *Paul and the Power of Grace*, 29, Kindle edition.

6. Barclay, *Paul and the Power of Grace*, 30, Kindle edition.

7. Barclay, *Paul and the Power of Grace*, 30, Kindle edition.

efficacy. "Gifts that achieve something, that change things for the better, might be regarded as better than gifts with limited positive effect."[8] Giving someone the change in my pocket is one thing; the person may go and spend it on a bag of chips. Giving students a second chance to take an exam on which they cheated is another. The students may have a change of heart that affects their future behavior. Sixth is *noncircularity*, and this is the element that Barclay argues we've taken up in the modern west. "Western modernity," he writes, "is inclined to perfect the gift as 'pure' only when there is no reciprocity, no return or exchange."[9] He goes on to show that this is a very recent development in the understanding of gifts, since gifts in antiquity were always given in relationships, where some reciprocity was expected to show appreciation, and thus to further or sustain that relationship.

These are all "perfections" of gifts. They're ways in which gifts might be made "better," but we all know that most of our giving falls well short of these standards. Our motives are often mixed. We give to those whom we think deserve it, and we seldom give lavishly. Still, keeping these facets of "the perfect gift" in mind will help us in the pages ahead, as we examine who God is, what he's done, and how he makes us into givers who reflect him.

In alignment with these perfections, Barclay's simplified definition of a gift is "the sphere of voluntary, personal relations characterized by goodwill in the giving of a benefit

---

8. Barclay, *Paul and the Power of Grace*, 31, Kindle edition.

9. Barclay, *Paul and the Power of Grace*, 31, Kindle edition.

or favor, which generally elicits some form of reciprocal return that is necessary for the continuation of the relationship."[10]

With this groundwork laid, let's move into our discussion of God as the grand Giver and the circular nature of giving.

---

10. Barclay, *Paul and the Power of Grace*, 17, Kindle edition.

The Triune Giver

FATHER   SON
Giver   Receiver

SPIRIT
Gift

"For he whom God has sent utters the words of God,
for he gives the Spirit without measure." John 3:34

Chapter 1

The candlelight flickers on the wall. It's not yet dawn. September is the time of the crickets, when they make their leg-songs in the humble dark. In a few months, it will be the time of silence, when the cold of winter hushes the world to a whisper. In the cricket calls and the silence, God is there. He is *here*, with you as you read. And he is giving.

He is giving the crickets. He is giving the dark and the light as the earth turns its hunched shoulders towards and then away from the sun. He is giving the silence. And he is giving me these words. God is an incessant and prodigal Giver. But this goes beyond what God *does*. It's who he *is*.

Before Time

There's a traditional teaching on the Trinity from Saint Augustine that depicts the Father as giver, the Spirit as gift, and the Son as recipient.[1] The Holy Spirit is a *person* and a *gift*, given to the Son by the Father. And yet this "gift" imagery can also extend to the Father and Son. There's a sense in which the Father gives himself to the Son, showing him all that he does (John 5:20), and a sense in which the Son gives

---

1. Saint Augustine, *De Trinitate* 15.33–36.

himself to the Spirit and to the Father. The Son did, after all, wander into the desert in the power of the Spirit (Matt. 4), according to the will of his Father. Does that strike you as strange, that a person can give himself to another person? If it does, it's probably because we overlook the profound truth that giving *oneself* in love is the greatest gift—the handing over of all, in fullness, to another. Keeping nothing protected. Leaving nothing behind. Offering all in sweet, almost levitating abandon. This is so rare in the world that it sounds like holy fiction, an ideal no one can really practice.

But not so with God. God is a Giver. He gives himself to himself, which would be strange if there weren't three persons in the Godhead. Thank goodness there are: Father, Son, and Spirit. Each gives to each and each to all.

Abraham Kuyper wrote beautifully of this love and mutual self-giving. He called it God's "love-life."[2]

> The Love-life whereby these three mutually love each other is the eternal being Himself. This alone is the true and real life of love. The entire Scripture teaches that nothing is more precious and glorious than the Love of the Father for the Son, and of the Son for the Father, and of the Holy Spirit for both.[3]

He says that this truth is a deep and ancient song. "We

---

2. John Frame also talks of the mutual love in the Godhead in his *Systematic Theology: An Introduction to Christian Belief* (Phillipsburg, NJ: P&R, 2013), 480–81. I have also written about this in *The Speaking Trinity & His Worded World: Why Language Is at the Center of Everything* (Eugene, OR: Wipf & Stock, 2018), 24–29.

3. Abraham Kuyper, *The Work of the Holy Spirit*, trans. Henri De Vries (Chattanooga, TN: AMG, 1995), 542.

listen to its music and adore it."[4]

Love is the greatest act of giving. It holds nothing back. All other gifts seem to let the giver retain something. Love requires open-armed abandon, complete vulnerability. For us, that's terrifying at times, but not so with God. Within that timeless triune community of love, there is unbroken and unhindered acceptance. This is only possible because God has one will. The Father, Son, and Spirit all want the same thing. They want each other, with love fiercer than fire, greater than any lover's gaze. I have not even the words to reach that place. But I know it's there, because God has told us it's there. It's who he is (1 John 4:8).

Love is the greatest act of giving.

God's self-love burns bright and glorious, like a great star set in a navy night sky. Jesus tells us this. "Father, glorify me with the glory I had with you before the world began" (John 17:5). Before the world began, in the stillness and the silence, there was the burning and beautiful glory of love, the illuminating hearth of self-giving. Jesus seems to allude to this when he says, "For he whom God has sent utters the words of God, for he [the Father] gives the Spirit without measure. The Father loves the Son and has given all things into his hand" (John 3:34–35). God gives the Spirit to the Son without measure, and because of the Father's great love, he even gives "all things" to him. He puts them *into his*

---

4. Kuyper, *The Work of the Holy Spirit*, 542.

hand. What a portrait of reception: the Father giving all to the Son in the Spirit.

And because elsewhere in Scripture we see that the love among the persons of the Trinity is reciprocal (John 14:31; Rom. 5:5; 1 John 4:8), we can say that the persons of the Trinity are always giving themselves to each other in love.[5] In fact, Jesus says that *it is because of his self-giving* that the Father loves him: "For this reason the Father loves me, because I lay down my life that I may take it up again" (John 10:17). In the giving, the Father loves the Son, for giving is simply who God is. This is God's *giving circle*.

> Radiant, the glory of giving,
> Father, Son, and Spirit each to each.
> A love unuttered by the living,
> A giving that God would bend and teach.

This feels so far from us, doesn't it? In order to even glimpse it, we have to hear a perfect high note on a violin or a holy pause between piano keys—and then we can follow that beauty like a tightrope. If we balance long enough, then maybe we see a glow on the dark horizon. Maybe. But it's there. It must be. As the Romanian theologian Dumitru Stăniloae once wrote, "The Holy Trinity is the supreme mystery of existence. It explains everything, and nothing can be explained without it."[6] Only the holy and eternal

---

5. Vern S. Poythress, *The Mystery of the Trinity: A Trinitarian Approach to the Attributes of God* (Phillipsburg, NJ: P&R, 2020), 564–65.

6. Dumitru Stăniloae, *The Holy Trinity: In the Beginning There Was Love*, trans. Roland Clark (Brookline, MA: Holy Cross Orthodox Press, 2012), xi.

giving of God could explain the great power of giving—the way something inside us releases when we give to others, the way clouds clear in the sky of the soul when we see that it's not about us. It's never been. Givers at heart are never concerned for themselves. They trust the great power of God to care for them, to receive them, and to carry them home.

Why? Because they know that giving is circular, that givers are also receivers and gifts, and that God has invited us into his circle of self-giving. In that circle, no one is ultimately left uncared for; everyone is given, gives, and receives.

This, dear friends, is *The Book of Giving*, and so it must begin with the God who gives. And it must end there, too.

The Self-Giving God

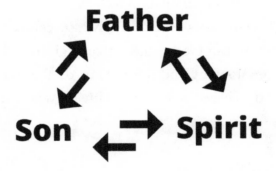

PRAYER

God, you are the great Giver.
You know giving not just with us,
But with yourself.
When we give, we image you.
But we long to grasp things in the world.
Help us to see what we can release.
Help us to watch the world
With open hands, ready to hold out
Whatever you have given us.

REFLECTION QUESTIONS

1.   How does the truth of God as a giver change the
way you see him and the gospel?
2.   How does God as the Great Giver change the way
you see yourself in relation to him?
3.   This emphasis on God as giver reveals certain things
about him. But God is more than a giver. He's also just,
wise, omnipotent, and so on. How do these other facets
of God's character interact with the truth of God as
giver?

Reader Resource: The Giving Checklist

God gives himself to himself, but we'll soon see how much God gives of himself to us. We often forget these gifts of God; we may not even perceive them as gifts. But there are gifts of knowledge, the great gift of salvation, the gift of relationships, and so on. Let's start by taking stock of the gifts you possess right now from the self-giving God. How many gifts can you express in the categories below? Think about how you possess them uniquely. Then write out a prayer of thanks for each one. I offer an example in the first row.[7] For additional discussion, consider how each gift reflects the six "perfections" of gifts that Barclay presents in *Paul and the Power of Grace* (superabundance, singularity, priority, noncircularity, efficacy, and incongruity).

The Gifts of God	Your Unique Possession	Your Prayer of Thanks
Knowledge of who God is	*I know that God is three persons in one, and he calls me into communion with him so that I can forever speak with the Father, Son, and Spirit.*	*God, thank you for revealing who you are to me, so that I can know you personally and long to be in fellowship with you each and every day.*
Knowledge of who you are		
The salvation of your soul		

---

7. To get a printable version of this, go to http://piercetaylorhibbs.com/the-book-of-giving-reader-resources/.

The Gifts of God	Your Unique Possession	Your Prayer of Thanks
Your family relationships		
Your friends		
Your possessions		
Your shelter		
Your food		
Your body		
Your memory		

Chapter 2

Think of a cup overflowing with water, the edges rounded over by the substance streaming down the sides. There's too much, in a beautiful way; the abundance is glorious, for what could be greater than free fullness, than a basin of blessing running over?

That's a picture of creation. But in this chapter, we're only looking at a part of it, at the crown jewel. We're looking at you.

God has something in himself, something we have called "life." It's hard to define, though we might call it *wakeful presence*, an alert and open appreciation simply for being.

We see pictures of it in the world around us. Rose buds ready to break into beauty, song sparrows flitting and hopping through the grass, collared dogs driving their owners down the street—noses full of scents from dirt and dry leaves. The wakeful presence of the world.

But that's mysteriously different from the sort of wakeful presence you see in the mirror each morning. There, as eyes look into eyes, you see what God describes as an image of himself. And it's beautiful.

David Whyte writes that "beauty is the harvest of

presence."[1] I had to think about that for a while, but then something clicked. Harvest: the gathering together; presence: the quality of being truly and fully here. Yes . . . beauty is a gathering of what is truly and fully here. Sometimes we notice it; many times we don't. That's why perceiving something beautiful can sometimes make us feel a bit sad. We want the world to see what we see, and we want it to be seen forever. But we know that many have not and will not see it. Or we know that it's passing, so they won't get the chance to.

> ## *We want the world to see what we see,*
> ## *and we want it to be seen forever.*

But *you*—you are beautiful in a way that goes beyond time and human memory. You have this life in you, this wakeful presence, uniquely. And it's unique because it comes from the breath of God. "Then the LORD God formed the man of dust from the ground and breathed into his nostrils the breath of life, and the man became a living creature" (Gen. 2:7). *God-breath*—that's what you have in you. Go ahead. Take in some more. Enjoy your oxygen. It's a gift of greatness from the God of life, the God who is life, the God who brought you into his giving circle.

Abraham Kuyper wrote that "a thing lives if it moves

---

1. David Whyte, *Consolations: The Solace, Nourishment, and Underlying Meaning of Everyday Words* (Langley, WA: Many Rivers, 2018), 19.

from within."[2] From within—something on the inside (the soul) animates the outside. The inside, the living soul, is a breath-gift from the Giver. And every gift is one-of-a-kind. Yet all of them reflect the same Giver (Eph. 4:1–16). We all carry within us "a breath of life from above."[3]

And so you carry the gift around in your lungs, walking through the world with a present in your chest. It goes with you into every syllable, every muscle movement, every thought—through the sweet smell of the summer grass and the touch of another person's skin. You always carry the gift.

The question goes deeper than what you'll do with this breath-gift of God. It goes to a strange place: will you give it *back* to him? That's the real question at the heart of life.

Jesus said, "It is more blessed to give than to receive" (Acts. 20:35). Certainly, he spoke about the daily acts of giving we can offer. But what propels those acts is a deeper longing to do what Jesus would do, what the Trinity has always done: give *yourself*, to hold on to nothing in your will and simply smile at the acceptance of another, the embrace of yourself by someone else. That's what Eugene Peterson meant when he said,

> Giving is what we do best. It is the air into which we are born. It is the action that was designed into us before our birth. Giving is the way the world is. God

---

2. Abraham Kuyper, *The Work of the Holy Spirit*, trans. Henri De Vries (Chattanooga, TN: AMG, 1995), 293.

3. Herman Bavinck, *The Wonderful Works of God: Instruction in the Christian Religion according to the Reformed Confession*, trans. Henry Zylstra (Glenside, PA: Westminster Seminary Press, 2019), 193.

gives himself. He also gives away everything that is. He makes no exceptions for any of us. We are given away to our families, to our neighbors, to our friends, to our enemies—to the nations. Our life is for others.[4]

We can do this self-giving on the human level with our deepest relationships. For instance, I would gladly give myself to my wife and to my children. My joy is *their* joy. If giving up my will for their good brings them happiness, I'll do it (though not without the inner struggle that comes from the old sinful self).[5] I keep trying to do it, as the Spirit— my breath-giver—leads me. And I trip over myself along the way. Selfishness is a stone we place at our own feet. It trips us, and it weighs us down when we try to carry it on our backs. It's burdensome. As Kelly Kapic put it, "We live under the burden and illusion of self-ownership."[6]

Selfishness is a stone we place at our own feet. It trips us, and it weighs us down when we try to carry it on our backs.

4. Eugene Peterson, *Run with the Horses: The Quest for Life at Its Best*, commemorative ed. (Downers Grove, IL: IVP Books, 2019), 42–43.

5. Paul Miller talks about this relinquishing of self-will as part of what he calls the J-curve. The J-curve represents the dying of our will and the humble self-giving that mirrors Jesus's life. Following that descent into death is resurrection life, again mirroring what happened to Christ. I have found Miller's J-curve to be a wonderful tool in searching for opportunities to give myself for others. See Paul E. Miller, *J-Curve: Dying & Rising with Jesus in Everyday Life* (Wheaton, IL: Crossway, 2019).

6. Kelly M. Kapic, *The God Who Gives: How the Trinity Shapes the Christian Story* (Grand Rapids, MI: Zondervan, 2018), 19, Kindle edition.

But the great sea current of Scripture moves us even beyond this. It asks us if we will give ourselves back to *God.* And while we certainly can do this *through* giving ourselves to others, that's not the end of it.

Eventually, as I had to watch my father do when I was eighteen, we give our breath-gift back to God. The breath-gift has a timeline. We don't get to keep it forever (though we will get something more amazing when we finally give it up). We give it back to the Giver. As Peterson wrote, "We are going to have to give up our lives finally, and the longer we wait the less time we have for the soaring and swooping life of Grace."[7]

The breath-gift we have is bound to be given back. That doesn't mean it's not a real gift. If someone gives you a book to read and then asks for it back after you've read it, that's still a gift. The gift is not in the *keeping;* it's in the *receiving.* Ultimately, we do not truly keep any of the gifts others give us (except for the gift of life that God has given). We're finite, and the gifts we have go with us only so far. We borrow them. And the breath-gift of God is the ultimate borrow.

Returning the breath-gift of God is a momentous occasion, but it's not a loss. It feels that way, as we watch others bow out from the land of the living. It feels final. And it is in a sense. But in another sense, it isn't.

That other sense lives on top of God's promise mountain. It's the promise of *with.* It's the promise of communion. And that promise is far better, in the end, than earthly breath in

---

7. Peterson, *Run with the Horses,* 43.

a broken world.

Understand this: As we've wandered over the hills of history since our ancient beginning, we've confused something. We've confused *life* and *time*. You and I seem bent on thinking that life *is* time. That's why we always want more of it. But life is not time. Life is God. That's why the second person of the Trinity stood upon the earth and boldly spoke a simple truth: "I am the way, the truth, and the life" (John 14:6). Life isn't time; life is a person. It's a relationship. Life is communion with the God who *is* life.

Giving back our breath-gift means we trade a shadow for a reality, a whisper for a voice, a candle for the sun. Giving back our life is gaining true and eternal life with the God who beckons us into fellowship.

> *Giving back our breath-gift means we trade a shadow for a reality, a whisper for a voice, a candle for the sun.*

So, even our giving back is another gift to be received. Remember, giving is circular.

This amazing gift of Spirit-life, the thing you hold in your chest right now, was superseded by God giving us himself in a way no one could have imagined, an eternal act of giving that brings us into eternal fellowship with the eternal God. That's where we go next.

PRAYER

God of giving,
I try to possess.
I try to grasp and not let go.
I cling to things with my self-will.
Selfishness runs in my blood.
But you have given me new blood,
Your blood.
And that blood is the blood of giving.
You call me to give myself away.
Open my ears to that call today.
Help me to know when and how to give.
Move my heart and hands to action.
Make me a mirror of Christ.

REFLECTION QUESTIONS

1. What are some of the ways in which you assert your self-will on a daily basis?
2. What are some of the ways in which you give yourself to others?
3. When you give yourself to another, how does that make you feel?
4. What things in your life seem to make you want to possess your breath-gift and never give it up? In other words, what things make you feel opposed to giving your life back to God?

Reader Resource: The Self-Will Survey

We're all prone to protect and assert our will. That's part of what it means to be in a glass world fractured by sin. But this habit keeps us from giving. It tightens the fist of our life, hiding our gifts behind white knuckles. Below is a little survey you can take to become more self-aware. Self-awareness, after all, is the first step toward change. In this case, it's the first step in becoming a more prodigal giver. Answer the questions in the left column, adding some comments in the middle if you like. Be honest. Then consider an opportunity for giving in that area. Intentionality is key. If you're intentional about becoming a greater giver, God's Spirit will work to make it happen. I've given an example in the first row. It would be good to revisit this survey periodically to see how you're changing and growing. There's always more to work on.[8]

Area of Life	Often/Sometimes/ Never	Giving Opportunity
I assert my self-will with my personal schedule.	*Often. I tend to take care of my own tasks before I take care of others.*	*Breakfast. Make your kids' breakfast BEFORE you make your own. Do the same for your wife.*
I assert my self-will in my relationships with family.		
I assert my self-will in my relationships with friends.		

---

8. To get a printable version of this, go to http://piercetaylorhibbs.com/the-book-of-giving-reader-resources/.

Area of Life	Often/Sometimes/Never	Giving Opportunity
I assert my self-will in my spiritual development.		
I assert my self-will in the care of my body.		

Chapter 3

Ours is a world of radishes and rainbows, wood grains and water bugs, leaky buckets and burning trees. Ours is a world of smoke and ice, rose petals and self-portraits. Here, we get splinters and sweat, mosquito bites and muscle tears. Snow has a soft sting and rain a piercing prick.

This is a place of effort. Fifty leaves churn out energy to make a single apple. Flowers spend hours holding up their heads in hope of rain. Fathers say a hundred *don'ts* before a son nods in assent. Weeds are drawn in masses so that basil can thrive; we pull water from the ground for our greenery when the windows of heaven are closed.

And we are small and fragile here, against the rolling mountains in the sea and the rocky cliffs that nudge the sky, beneath the stars that burn from a billion miles and the planets strolling in circles.

Into this place, *this* place, the Giver came. He was always here, of course (Ps. 139:7–12), hovering over and sustaining all with his quiet speech (Heb. 1:3). He's ever present. And yet we could never put bone and flesh to him, not until an infant's breath parted the air on a starry night two thousand years ago. That was when the Giver gave what even our dreams couldn't reach.

The first great gift we received was the breath-gift from God's own Spirit. The second was a shape we knew—someone we could touch and see and smell. Someone we could hear.

It's hard to grasp how a *person* can be a gift. But from God's perspective, this must have seemed beautifully obvious. As we already noted, he's been giving the gift of persons since eternity, Father to Son and Son to Father; Spirit to Son and Son to Spirit; Spirit to Father and so on—the wondrous open-palmed life of the Godhead.

The gift of Christ could not have been dreamed by us, but it was a gift flowing from the very nature of God, the master of whole, unreserved person-giving. The giving of Christ is what opened the door for humanity to enter God's giving circle.

The gift of Christ could not have been dreamed by us, but it was a gift flowing from the very nature of God, the master of whole, unreserved person-giving.

And so the eternal Son entered our world of beetles and breaths, stones and silence, voices and vision. He entered. And he stayed.

Every second of his waking day, every exhalation of midnight air, every finger movement and vocal cord vibration was a gift, for this was truly Immanuel, the *with-*

us God. Every glorious day in his earthly life was packed and wrapped and ribboned for us. People drew back the paper of his life moment by moment, wholly unaware of what they were receiving at first—that this was *God* given for them. Christ was the walking God-gift, coming to *us*, meeting *us*, seeking *us* out. Yes, Christ is the gift who seeks out his recipients. This is what John Barclay means when he says that a perfect gift retains *priority*. It goes first, before any act could call for it. And no gift is higher than this in terms of efficacy. When we accept the gift of Christ, it changes everything. It replaces our heart. It gives us new life, with eyes to see and ears to hear.

Now, Christ's giving went on for some thirty-three years. And then, when the time had ripened like a rose bud, he prepared himself to be consumed, a gift fully taken and not given back (recall Barclay's notion of noncircularity).

> Now as they were eating, Jesus took bread, and after blessing it broke it and gave it to the disciples, and said, "Take, eat; this is my body." And he took a cup, and when he had given thanks he gave it to them, saying, "Drink of it, all of you, for this is my blood of the covenant, which is poured out for many for the forgiveness of sins. (Matt. 26:26–28)

He tore the bread, as his body would be torn. And, as his whole life was a gift all along, he gave it away. They ate tiny pieces of him in a room filled with firelight.[1] He went down

---

1. Doctrinally, I agree with the Reformed tradition's take on a symbolic understanding of the sacraments. However, I feel that we need to think through this with pictorial language so that the meaning soaks into our hearts.

to their insides, into their stomachs, and then the nutrients went into their blood. And that's where he wanted to live: on the inside, deep in the recesses of their being, beckoning from their blood with the song of self-giving. They took in the Giver *in order to become givers* (though, they may not have known the latter part). As I said earlier, *this* is how we entered God's giving circle. When we enter that circle, we don't just *believe* more; we *become* more. We conform to the nature of the self-giving God.

They took in the Giver in order to become givers.

Then came the wine. His body had already been given. He lived in their blood. But now—Gift of gifts!—*his* insides would greet *their* insides; his blood would mingle with theirs. The holy Gift of God himself poured out in the open air of every human soul. How could this happen? Really, I'm asking. I'm marveling with you. *How could this happen?*

And do you smell it? Christ's blood has the scent of forgiveness, the soul-spice of sacrifice, calling wrongs to be righted, bent thoughts to be straightened, false hopes to be let go, and fingers to unfurl. It is the gift of the Giver that *makes* us givers. God's gift *did* something to us. It changed us. It made us the Giver's possession, his inheritance. As M.

Douglas Meeks once wrote, "God owns by giving."[2] And when God possesses us, he changes us, making us more like himself.

Who could have imagined this blood-gift, the rawness and the red, the mockery of God for the marrow of men?

Who could have imagined this blood-gift, the rawness and the red, the mockery of God for the marrow of men?

This gift of the Son goes beneath all so that it can claim all; what Christ did began an unstoppable and holistic redemption—a redemption that not only includes us but also the world in which we live: the radishes and the rainbows, the wood grains and the water bugs, the snow and the rain, for creation itself was waiting for this gift—the revealing of the sons of God (Rom. 8:19). And it waits still, to be "set free from its bondage to corruption," to cling to "the glory of the children of God" (Rom. 8:21). Woven into the fabric of creation is an expectancy—a Christmas-colored anticipation of the gift *we* would receive. This is because God's gifts keep giving, just as God himself gives ceaselessly. The giving doesn't end; it flows forward. This,

---

2. M. Douglas Meeks, *God the Economist: The Doctrine of God and Political Economy* (Minneapolis, MN: Fortress, 1989), 115, quoted in Kelly M. Kapic, *The God Who Gives: How the Trinity Shapes the Christian Story* (Grand Rapids, MI: Zondervan, 2018), 17, Kindle edition. Kapic earlier wrote, "As we learn to dwell in the good news of belonging to God, we will grow in the freedom to give ourselves to God and others in ways that are impossible for those who treasure their lives as their own" (p. 12).

once again, is *the giving circle*, pictured below.[3] Your salvation and mine are lovingly celebrated by the rosebud. As a soul accepts Christ, the rose says, "Ah . . . soon this will be over: no more corruption." The leaf bug and the large-mouth bass both offer their amen. "One person closer," they say. "One person closer."

But even this, even *this* was not the end of God's person giving. Next would come the Holy Ghost and the evergreen indwelling of our Trinity.

The Giving Circle

3. John Barclay notes, "in most cultures and at most times, gifts are part of a circular exchange, an ongoing cycle where the gift is intended to create or maintain a social relationship. . . . One gives or gives back (typically at a later time and in some nonidentical form) in order to continue a relationship that is in principle open-ended." *Paul and the Power of Grace* (Grand Rapids, MI: William B. Eerdmans, 2020), 17–18, Kindle edition.

PRAYER

God, how could you give us your Son?
How?
We don't know.
We don't understand.
Love is beyond reason.
It leaves reason at home
While it explores the wild,
Spending everything.
Lord, you spent everything on us.
Help me unwrap that gift of you,
Once more,
And stare at it.
Help me to believe the truth
That you are in me,
And that resurrection
Is my reality
And my destiny.
Then lead me to give.
Help me put my feet
In your footprints.

REFLECTION QUESTIONS

1. How does God show his love for us?
2. Why do you think it can be easy for us to belittle the great gift of God's Son and focus on lesser joys?
3. What do you think the gift of God's Son should

prompt you to do?

4. Why does giving seem so hard for us at times?

Reader Resource: A Giving Poem

Sometimes we need truth to be lyrical for it to sink into our souls. That's why we all remember children's songs fifty years after we hear them. "Jesus loves me. This is I know, for the Bible tells me so." Below is a poem you might memorize to help you keep the truth of God's great gift close to your heart. May it lead you to give yourself to others as well, as the Spirit fills you with the life that others so desperately need.

The Giver

Ancient, great, and evergreen,
God gives himself away.
And we receive him now unseen
With every dawning day.

The Son is true and real and good.
The Father always gives
So that we give back, as we should,
The life that truly lives.

Chapter 4

The ancient breath-gift you hold in your lungs right now, lending oxygen to your blood stream, was the first gift you received when your body was pushed into the world from the womb of your mother, glazed in her blood, greeting the light and sound. You came into this world of footsteps and candlewicks, tables and chairs, buttons and blankets. The breath-gift of God's Spirit gave you *all*. It sits beneath you every movement, holding you up like a duck on a pond.

But that gift was never meant to be the end. It's a gift for the body. It allows room for the soul to sprout and grow into its God-given identity. Yet ours is a broken world, a place where the breath-gift is not just neglected; far worse— it's forgotten. And gifts forgotten never have the chance to serve their purpose.

Gifts forgotten never have the chance to serve their purpose.

To shepherd us through a broken world, after the great gift of God's own Son, yet another gift was given, another person of the Godhead: the Spirit. Two holy and eternal persons gift-wrapped and set before every human soul—this is Christmas unending.

The gift of the Spirit is beautifully strange. The wrapping paper doesn't tear or crinkle. It just loosens and falls away. He sets himself before us in glorious silence. He enters into us and quietly takes the nice seat in the corner.

But that takes nothing from his potency, for the Spirit is the touch of God. Abraham Kuyper wrote, "The Father remains outside of the creature; the Son touches him outwardly; by the Holy Spirit the divine life touches him directly in his inward being."[1] A direct touch . . .

Of course, Kuyper knew that this divine touch would make way for the Father and Son to enter the threshold of our souls. That's why Jesus can say, "If anyone loves me, he will keep my word, and my Father will love him, and we will come to him and make our home with him" (John 14:23). A home for the Trinity—think of it! Every human soul can house four persons: himself, and the Father, Son, and Spirit. But more on that in a moment.

Because the Spirit comes so quietly, because the wrapping paper falls away without a sound, we may hardly notice it at first. And as the Spirit is light on his wind-borne feet (John 3:8), we can get in a sad habit of not noticing him, of assuming he isn't with us, or even of thinking his presence doesn't make much of a difference.

How do we notice him? First stillness, and then a growing awareness of what "life" really is. I was reminded by Marilyn

---

1. Abraham Kuyper, *The Work of the Holy Spirit*, trans. Henri De Vries (Chattanooga, TN: AMG, 1995), 45.

McEntyre recently,

> When our interior spaces are filled with plans, anxieties, curiosities, even the morning's news or good intentions, we leave little room for the Spirit to enter. The Spirit of the Lord may "blow where it will," but the force of that mighty wind may be diminished by the obstacles we put in its path. The Spirit may blow us over, but most often, it seems to me, it weaves its way quietly, courteously, and subtly through the scattered minutes of an ordinary day. [2]

We stuff ourselves every day. We pack in the longings and loves, the doubts and dreams, the fears and failures. And then we pour in the water of information—a constant deluge. Is it any wonder that our awareness of the Spirit's holy wind is lost? Finding and feeling that wind again is a matter of stillness. "Be still and know that I am God" (Ps. 46:10), wrote the psalmist. Knowledge follows on the coattails of stillness. The still, small voice comes after the tearing winds and the shaking ground and the raging fire (1 Kgs. 19:11–12). It's stillness that ushers in a noticing of God's Spirit.

Knowledge follows on the coattails of stillness.

After the stillness, or in the midst of it, comes the awareness of what life really is. It's not the intake of

---

2. Marilyn McEntyre, *Word by Word: A Daily Spiritual Practice* (Grand Rapids, MI: William B. Eerdmans, 2016), 129.

oxygen or the animation of the body. It's something deeper. Something at the bottom of the well. As we noted in a previous chapter, life is an ever-giving, ever-present, ever-open and offering *person*. Jesus says that *he* is the life (John 14:6). And so life at its foundation must be a relationship.

Life is an ever-giving, ever-present, ever-open and offering person.

When we think about the meaning of our own lives, we think about the relationships, the ones whom we witness and who witness us. Writing about friendship, David Whyte says,

> The ultimate touchstone of friendship is not improvement, neither of the other or of the self, the ultimate touchstone is witness, the privilege of having been *seen* by someone and the equal privilege of being granted the sight of the essence of another, to have walked with them and to have believed in them, and sometimes just to have accompanied them for however brief a span, on a journey impossible to accomplish alone.[3]

It's the witness that bleeds into our grasp of what our life really is.

My life is the witness of my mother, in her constant care for me and my three brothers, and in our response to her,

---

3. David Whyte, *Consolations: The Solace, Nourishment, and Underlying Meaning of Everyday Words* (Langley, WA: Many Rivers, 2018), 74.

in the thousand table-settings, in the words of affirmation and correction, in the touch of her skin and the pulsing intentions of her heart toward us and ours toward her.

My life is the witness of my father, in his shepherding gaze and our watchful seeking of direction, in the rub of his thick black beard against our hairless little necks, in the sound of his voice in the echo of our own, in his brown-eyed stare from a cancer bed and ours back to him, in the witness of the rock marking where we laid his body in the earth, in our witness of each other before the sealed door of mortality.

My life is the witness of my brothers and theirs of me, in the tennis balls thrown and the corn slung at each other while autumn sighed to an ending, in the rising facial muscles and unbound music of laughter.

My life is the witness of my wife, in her green-eyed beauty and grace, in the softness of her skin and hair, in her constant thought and behavior bending around me and mine around her. It's in the passion of our eyes for each other, and the sympathy that comes from souls rubbing shoulders day after day.

My life is the witness of my kids, in their wild wonder at the sound of their own voices and their ever-widening imaginations, in the knowledge my forearms bear from holding them up and my lips from kissing their cheeks.

My life is a witness to relationships. And so is yours.

My life is a witness to relationships.
And so is yours.

But beneath all of our human relationships, bearing them up and giving them meaning amidst the threats of finality, is *him*. Our lives are about relationships because life is a relationship—the person of the Son, ever-bound to his Father, ever-bound to his Spirit. The one who gave his life is relationship. And that is why we're always drawn deeper than our human relationships. Relational life goes well beneath us. That's the only reason we can swim in the pools of rippling human relationships. That's also the reason why "gifts are a means of creating and sustaining relationships."[4] The giving circle of God points us simultaneously to the God who gives and the God who is love. Remember John's simplicity in this? "For God so *loved* the world, that he *gave . . .*" (John 3:16). The self-giving, loving God is the relationship beneath all of our relationships.

When we sense this, even in some visceral understanding of our own limitation and brevity, we sense the Spirit, the gift given to every believer. He's the one constantly at work drawing us nearer to the Son, reminding us of all he's said (John 14:26). He's the one witnessing us and calling us to witness to *him*, like the oriole ever working to weave a nest from the elements right in front of us. The Spirit constantly gathers our grass-clipping thoughts and the flower-bud intentions from the wild fields of the heart. He's always building, showing us the next place to rest, the next place to sleep, the next place from which we'll greet the warm morning light of another day. The Spirit gives himself to us

---

4. John Barclay, *Paul and the Power of Grace* (Grand Rapids, MI: William B. Eerdmans, 2020), 18, Kindle edition.

in gifts of perspective and awareness and love.

And the Spirit, as gift, gives a special bundle of gifts, too. The gifts he gives help us to enter and thrive in God's giving circle. How do we thrive in that circle? We thrive by reflecting the Great Giver, by giving ourselves to others in such a way that turns their chins toward the almighty. That's the subject of the next chapter.

PRAYER

> Spirit, you are a silent Giver.
> I don't sense you all the time,
> But I know you're quietly working,
> Always building and shaping and reminding.
> You call me back into relationship
> With the God who is a relationship.
> You bear me up when I am weak.
> You lift my head above the waves
> And turn my eyes toward light.
> Help me to rest on you,
> And to trust your carrying.

REFLECTION QUESTIONS

1. What has your experience been with the work of the Spirit? Think of a particular example if you can.
2. How has the Spirit helped you focus on relationships?
3. In what ways does the gift of God's Spirit continue to grant you new life and shape you to the image of

Christ?

4. What is a way in which you'd like to see the Spirit work in your life right now? Stop and pray for that. You might even write out your prayer, if that helps. Then track the answering.

Reader Resource: Who Is the Spirit?

Many people have difficulty identifying the Holy Spirit as a person. He seems more like a mist or a cloud without a face. But Scripture is clear that the Holy Spirit is a divine person of the Godhead, and it treats him as such.[5] Look up each of the passages below and write down what you learn about the Spirit as a person of the Godhead.[6]

Scripture Passage	What You Learn about the Spirit
John 16:7	
Acts 8:29	
Acts 13:2	
Rom. 8:14	

---

5. For details on this, see Robert Letham, *The Holy Trinity: In Scripture, History, Theology, and Worship*, revised and expanded ed. (Phillipsburg, NJ: P&R, 2019), 51–59; and John M. Frame, *Systematic Theology: An Introduction to Christian Belief* (Phillipsburg, NJ: P&R, 2013), 477–479.

6. These passages are taken from Don Stewart, "Is the Holy Spirit a Person?" Blue Letter Bible, accessed December 10, 2020, https://www.blueletterbible.org/faq/don_stewart/don_stewart_404.cfm.

Scripture Passage	What You Learn about the Spirit
Rom. 15:30	
Eph. 4:30	
1 Cor. 2:10	
1 Cor. 2:11	
1 Cor. 2:13	
Heb. 10:29	

Chapter 5

The Spirit gives many gifts. How poetic, since he himself is the Gift that God gives to the Son in perpetuity, the Gift he gives the Son without measure (John 3:34). In this chapter, we'll look not just at the gifts he gives, but at how each of those gifts is *relational* and *calls us to giving*. This again points out the circular nature of gifts—from God to us, from us to each other, from us back to God. "Gifts go round in circles."[1] We go to the classic text: Galatians 5:22–23. Get ready to soar on the broad wings of grace.

Love

The deepest and greatest gift—the one threaded through the heart of God—is love. What *is* love? I've heard it said that love is wanting the best for someone regardless of whether that involves you. There's truth to that. The man who lays down his life for his friends (John 15:13) leaves the world so that they can find themselves in it. Yet Scripture has a more cryptic (and potent) definition. Love is . . . *God* (1 John 4:8). That doesn't seem to be much of a definition, does it? But think about it.

1. John Barclay, *Paul and the Power of Grace* (Grand Rapids, MI: William B. Eerdmans, 2020), 22, Kindle edition.

As we've already seen, God is the Father giving himself to the Son, who gives himself back to the Father and Spirit, who gives himself back to the Son and the Father. God is the divine dance of person-giving. Below is a poem that came to me when I was thinking about this one morning.

Son to Father; Father to Son.
Spirit to each, and all are one.
The giving stays. It burns above
As the ever-giving God of love.

The gift of love, then, is the gift of God himself. The Spirit gives us this gift from the ancient dark, the gift that glowed reality into being.

How do you know you have this gift of the Spirit? For starters, the Spirit has already told you so. But you also know it more intimately by starting to move your muscles and joints to the melody of self-giving. And we can give ourselves to God in a host of ways. We'll get into this in the final section of the book. For now, we know that we can give our time and open ears as we listen to others, never saying a word. We can give our effort in making a meal for someone who just brought home an infant. We can give ourselves through words of encouragement and affirmation.

Notice that the gifts of love are colored by what they take from us and hold out to another. They are colored by *sacrifice*. In listening, we sacrifice our speech. In making a meal, we sacrifice the time we might spend on other tasks. In speaking words of encouragement, we sacrifice the desire to have those words spoken to us. Self-sacrifice is at the heart of love, and that's how you enter the dance.

> *The gifts of love are colored by what they take from us and hold out to another.*

Love, as the rest of the gifts of the Spirit, is relational at its core and calls us to self-giving. That's one of the reasons Paul can personify love so easily. "Love is patient and kind; love does not envy or boast; it is not arrogant or rude. It does not insist on its own way; it is not irritable or resentful; it does not rejoice at wrongdoing, but rejoices with the truth. Love bears all things, believes all things, hopes all things, endures all things" (1 Cor. 13:4–7). Do you see how he treats love as a person? That should make some sense by now, since the God who *is* three persons is also *love*. And so we see that *love*, *relationships*, and *self-giving* are bound up with one another.

Joy

Joy is often confused with happiness. The two are sisters. Joy is the elder, with memory in her skin. She is the deep and abiding contentment that brings our cheeks to rise in a smile. Jesus told his disciples about the details of his sacrifice and how his returning to the Father would be to their benefit. "These things I have spoken to you, that my joy may be in you, and that your joy may be full" (John 15:11). The Greek word used here for "joy" is the same for both Jesus's joy and our own. Jesus's joy is rooted in his love for the Father and in the unflinching reciprocation of that love. His joy lives in a *relationship*. Our joy thus lives in a relationship. And because that relationship doesn't end, our joy can't ultimately leave. We can be blinded to it, of course. We can *feel* joyless, but that doesn't mean the joy is gone. The joy has already been *given*; it's not taken away from us. Happiness, in contrast, comes and goes, flickering like a candlelight. It resembles the warmth of joy in its flame, but joy is the constantly burning hearth in winter—steady, certain, always warming up our bones when we gather around it.

When happiness leaves, joy stays. To switch metaphors, we might say that joy stays because it's rooted in more than yourself. Its roots climb down into the heart of God, who gave the gift. In contrast, happiness is the flowerhead—beautiful to look at and smell, but seasonal and fleeting on this side of eternity. Happiness travels, but joy makes its home in relationships.

Happiness travels, but joy makes its home in relationships.

In God's giving circle, we give joy to others by giving ourselves in relationship to them, by *staying* when happiness leaves, by *remaining* through the seasons and the years. Joy lives in marriages, aged through summers and winters. Joy lives in father and son, mother and daughter, and the legacy of a family, which matures from infancy to adulthood like a great tree. Joy lives in friendships that linger beyond conversations and banter. The joy of the self-giving God becomes the treasure of his self-giving people, a people who *stay*. That's how we enter the giving circle here. And remember, we can enter that circle only because of Christ, who *stayed* on the cross for us, who *stays* in our hearts at this very moment. We thrive in God's giving circle by embracing and then delivering the joy that Christ has given to us.

This joy lives in a home built upon God's love, the God-gift that supports all of the other God-gifts. And that home stands through the weather of happiness and sorrow. Joy, in short, is not so much something we chase as it is something that grows around and through us. We can be surrounded by it. As Marilyn McEntyre writes, "Joy is the objective, the hope, the evidence, and the outcome of a life lived in God's love, burning brilliant as gold in fire even in the very midst of sorrow."[2]

As with the Spirit's gift of love, the gift of joy is *relational* and calls us to *self-giving*. In other words, joy loosens our limbs so that we can dance in God's giving circle, pointing others to the joy that outlasts every song of happiness. Our joy is thus rooted in our relationship with the God who is love, and it's this God who encourages us to mirror that joy in the relationships all around us.

Peace

Peace is perhaps the most coveted gift of the Spirit, but we go after it for the wrong reasons. We search for it when

2. Marilyn McEntyre, *Word by Word: A Daily Spiritual Practice* (Grand Rapids, MI: William B. Eerdmans, 2016), 152.

our nerves are wracked, when turmoil squeezes the essence from our life like olives in an oil press, when we're dazed by distraction in a world of a thousand screams.

Peace, we think, is an absence, a ceasing of torment, a stilling of the waters. But peace is a presence. Peace is the presence of a person. "Peace I leave with you," Jesus said. "My peace I give you" (John 14:27). It's *his* peace, not *a* peace or the *feeling* of peace. And his peace is a relational peace, a calm ease trickling down the mountainside of divine relationship—with the Father who loves him (John 3:35) and the Spirit who loves and teaches from him (John 14:26). Peace lives in the Trinity. It lives among persons.

Peace is the presence of a person.

When Jesus says that he gives us his peace, he's saying that he gives us *himself*, all that he is and has done on our behalf. Peace is found in his person, in all its glorious richness, all of its Mediterranean skin and vibrating vocal cords, all of its sincere stares and healing touches, all of its cross-given splinters and thorn-drawn blood, all of its fullness from his resurrection hands. Peace is being united *with him, in him,* and thus being set right in the presence of our holy Father and his pulsing Spirit. Peace lives in our relationship with the Trinity.

And yet that peace given through relationship isn't something we sit on, like a cushion for the soul. It's something that must be passed on. This, again, is God's giving circle. We enter through Christ, and then by his Spirit *we* start giving ourselves to others and thus back to God, since giving ourselves to others is in accordance with God's will, who gave himself for us. As one of my favorite theologians put it, "God gives Himself to His people in order that His people should give themselves to Him."[3] Peace is meant to emerge from our hearts like a scent that drifts onto the paths of others. Peace is meant to be passed on, to be given. It is the prince of peace of who gave himself to us (Isa. 9:6). And as co-heirs with Christ, we pass on that peace to others.

But how can we give something like this to someone else? How do we work with peace in God's giving circle? The best we can do, I think, is become heralds. We can find little ways (ways which the Spirit will show us) to call out the coming of peace in the noisy marketplace of humanity. "Peace with God—lasting personal peace—is here! Come and see! God has come to dwell *in* us! Have you spoken to Peace today?" There is only one peace, found in the person of Christ. We can't give others any peace isolated from him.

We can also give peace by striving to speak and act with the goal of peace, behaving in the spirit of peace. This is often brought about with the affirmation of God's work in others.

Let me offer a personal example. I'm told I have an irenic presence, a calming presence. That's a strange thing to say about someone with an anxiety disorder.[4] But I think

---

3. Herman Bavinck, *The Wonderful Works of God: Instruction in the Christian Religion according to the Reformed Confession*, trans. Henry Zylstra (Glenside, PA: Westminster Seminary Press, 2019), 9.

4. I've written about this at length in *Struck Down but Not Destroyed: Living Faithfully with Anxiety* and *Finding Hope in Hard Things: A Positive Take on Suffering*.

this comes from a Spirit-sown longing to avoid conflict and live peaceably with others (Rom. 12:18). Something happens when that longing for peace dresses your words and actions. And people notice. But we have to remember that this Spirit-generated peace isn't some bare feeling or the absence of tangible suffering. It's the calm of persons in unending relationship. That's peace. It's a gift *from* persons (Father, Son, and Spirit) *to* persons. The persons of the Godhead have full and loving control of our lives. Laying your soul down in that truth, again and again, is what brings peace. Thinking, speaking, and acting from that place is how we can give peace to others.

> *Peace is a gift from persons (Father, Son, and Spirit) to persons.*

We see once more that God draws us into his giving circle by giving himself and then calling us to give from the endless reservoir of his own nature. Entering God's giving circle means entering a place of superabundance, a place that always offers us more than we could hope or imagine. When you think of it that way, how could we *not* focus on giving others what we've been given?

I'll pause here to apply what I've said to the transcultural crisis we're all acquainted with: the coronavirus pandemic. The pandemic will pass eventually, and some other evil will take its place. The world is broken, remember. And so while what I'm about to say pertains to our current situation, it will also be true for future crises.

We are running into walls of frustration because we seem bent on believing that peace is *only* a feeling. And if peace were only a feeling, then the best we could do is chase after it—spending all our intentions, time, and money on grasping it, like hands trying to grip a wisp of smoke. But if peace is ultimately a *person*, and not merely a feeling (though, we can still feel the presence of that person), then we're chasing after something false. The trouble, you see, isn't that we don't have peace. On the contrary, we have Christ, who *is* peace. It's not the feeling of peace that we need to chase after; it's *him*.

Practically, that means when we lack a *feeling* of peace, we need deeper and more sustained communion with the person of Christ. We need to bury our minds in God's Word and pray earnestly. We need to *speak* with him. We can read a million self-help books on how to "find lasting peace," but all that such books can do is lead to frustration. Why? Because they're focusing all their attention on the symptoms and not on the cure. They're trying to alleviate *feelings* without connecting us to the *person* who can give us what our souls most long for.

All that is to say, when you're feeling an absence of peace, you need the presence of Christ, not a positive self-image or an "abundance mindset." When we go through extreme anxiety and turmoil, what we need most is the *person* of peace. And it's only when we have *him* that we have anything of value to give to others who are struggling.

Forbearance

The next great gift of the Spirit is forbearance or patience. Forbearance is the gift of self-control married to time. We find it hard to be patient, both for events and for persons. There's an inner urge to move, to take, to judge. Forbearance is the gift of God's Spirit that says, "Wait, little one. Just wait." And God is the master of waiting. The Spirit waited to usher in the Son to a hurting world. The Father waited to send him. It would not happen until "the time had fully come" (Gal. 4:4). The waiting . . . through moments and hours and days and years and millennia. The waiting through curse and cut, insult and injury, loss and law-breaking. Such waiting.

Forbearance is the gift of self-control married to time.

The sending of the Son through the Spirit seems to be the greatest act of waiting, of forbearance. It was a forbearance with *people* in mind. When is the perfect moment to breech the curtains of a dark world with the light of healing? On a silent, starry night, in a stable with contented farm animals. Forbearance can lead to great surprises. But God's forbearance always has our good at heart (Rom. 8:28).

The trouble we encounter is often in keeping *persons* at the center of our Spirit-led forbearance. We want things— feelings, experiences, moments. But we have a hard time keeping persons in focus, either ourselves or others. This is what causes problems when we try to function in God's giving circle. God is always focused on *persons*, so when he invites us into his giving circle, that's the focus we should take on as well.[5] We need the Spirit for this, the divine person who can turn our chin with a hand of wind and direct our vision to the people in need, even as we're pressed by a groaning creation or a broken body to cling to the war of self-preservation.

The Spirit knows full well that persons are the jewels of God's speech, prisms of divine light. Because of how God made us, and how he re-made us in Christ, he knows what is worth waiting for, when forbearance must stand like a boulder in a rushing river, still and strong against the rapids.

Giving to others out of forbearance can take many forms. The most applicable is probably holding our tongue. We don't think of listening as a gift, but it is. It truly is. Patient listening is an ancient well from which we all draw. It deepens us as it offers space to another. The room we create in our own soul serves as a sitting room for the speaker. And this is no small gift.

Marilyn McEntyre writes of Mary listening to Jesus while Martha busied herself with tasks that surely seemed polite and necessary.

Among Jesus's female followers, one of the most beloved

---

5. There's a wealth of wisdom in the Christian notion of *Christian personalism*, which I've found not only in the work of Kenneth Pike and Vern Poythress, but also in the Reformed faith more broadly. For some background on this, see Pierce Taylor Hibbs, *The Trinity, Language, and Human Behavior: A Reformed Exposition of the Language Theory of Kenneth L. Pike*, Reformed Academic Dissertations (Phillipsburg, NJ: P&R, 2018), 160–163.

is Mary, whose listening—the "better part" she chose—lay at the heart of her participation in Jesus's life and ministry. Her story reminds us that it may be the quiet listeners among us who are harboring gifts greater than we imagine, gifts that sustain the life of the whole body.[6]

Yes, listening is a gift. And we have opportunities throughout each day to give that gift to others.

Why don't we? Why do we shut the window that gives fresh air to the thoughts of another? Sometimes it's out of a habit we've developed that's essentially self-centered. We spend the moments of listening just waiting for our turn to speak. And that's not listening. That's ignorance. We all do it—God, help us.

The gift of listening requires emptying. We have to pour out our good intentions, our self-affirmed "wisdom," our belief that what we might say is worth more than silence. We have to empty ourselves in an instant in order to make room for the words of another. In this, we step in the footpath of Christ, who emptied himself and was silent for us (Phil. 2:5–8; Isa. 53:7). In the Godhead, the Word is heard in full. As children of that Word, we also leave room for the words of others. We make space for hearing.

> There is a space for the Word among Father and Spirit.
> He is heard. He is taken. He is seen.
> So we leave room for words in silence. Can you hear it?
> They're embraced. They're acknowledged. They are free.

---

6. McEntyre, *Word by Word*, 9.

Kindness

Kindness requires creativity. We have to witness the world and the people in it as boats with open sails, ready to be pushed by the wind of thoughtfulness. God, to my amazement, has put this power in our hands. And so this, too, is a gift we give to others. As with the other gifts of the Spirit, it's relational, interpersonal. It's a gift that helps us thrive in God's giving circle.

Kindness requires creativity.

Ian Maclaren once wrote, "Be kind, for every man is fighting a hard battle." Kindness emerges from an awareness of and compassion for others. To be kind, we must crawl out of the hermit crab shell of selfishness and truly see someone else. And then comes the giving—the soft wind in the sail of another.

It's often easy and yet breath-taking to witness kindness in children. One of my kids made me a bookmark as a kindergarten project. On the front are three pictures, where "I love you" is depicted in sign language. On the back is a picture of me, drawn and colored in crayon wax. My child made this for me when we were apart. Why? Why bend and color with little fingers a portrait of daddy in crayon wax? Sitting in a room full of children and a teacher, my child thought of *me* and worked to produce a laminated testament of love, of kindness. Why? Because the Holy Spirit was kindling kindness in my child's heart. Such a pure and passionate gift could only have its origins in God. That bookmark is a precious act of kindness. I keep it in my Bible and look at it every morning. It never fails to put a little wind in my sails.

My kids also have a deep emotional intelligence, alerting them to someone else's pain or pleasure whenever they share a room with others. I can't tell you how many times they've wandered over to my leg and hugged me when they sense my frustration or sadness. It's a kindness that goes straight to my bones.

Kindness was made to be given. God is the source; we are the wielders. Through us his Spirit flows like water, a current constantly asking the soul to give.

Goodness

The word "good" is a pebble in our world, always kicked around in conversations, but we don't stop to pick it up and examine it. What does it even mean to be "good"?

As with the other gifts of the Spirit, this is a relational thing, meant to be extended to others. But we start with God, the source of the gift, the one who invites us into his giving circle.

Goodness is personal because God *is* good, and God is three persons in one essence. Goodness, in that sense, is a synonym for God-ness or godliness. To be good is to be like God.

But how is *God* good? What does that mean? Note first that language is webs within webs, words linked and sewn to other words.[7] If we want to know what "good" means

---

7. Kenneth Pike would say it's "wheels within wheels," but the principle is the same.

in relation to God, we have to tread the spider's silk to other words.

Most theologians I've read say that for God to be good means that he is *beautiful, lovely*, and *purposeful*.[8] And surely this is true for the persons of the Godhead. Jesus himself said, "The Father loves the Son and has given all things into his hand" (John 3:35). And that love went beyond "the foundation of the world" (John 17:4). And the Son loves the Father and abides in that love (John 15:10). He lives there. And so does the Holy Spirit, for the fruit he produces is love (Gal. 5:22). There is a house of divine love . . .

And because God is perfect, his love is perfect, and perfect love is intentional, purposeful. God does not accidentally love himself. His self-love in the Trinity is always known and measured, seen and sent, wrapped and received. God is Christmas, ever giving the gift of himself to himself. He has built the house where goodness lives, where loveliness and beauty talk eternally on the front porch.[9]

God is Christmas, ever giving the gift of himself to himself.

We enter that holy circle of goodness by divine invitation. And so for us goodness fits into analogous categories, each taking their shape from God. As the Spirit bears the fruit

8. See, for instance, Herman Bavinck, *God and Creation*, v. 2 of *Reformed Dogmatics*, ed. John Bolt, trans. John Friend (Grand Rapids, MI: Baker, 2004), 210–213.

9. On the Son as the source of all beauty in our world, see Pierce Taylor Hibbs, "Beauty Embodied," Reformation21, February 5, 2016, https://www.reformation21. org/articles/beauty-embodied.php.

of goodness in our hearts, we take up the love, beauty, and purposes of God for the benefit of others. This gift of the Spirit, as with the other gifts, is relational. It's meant to be passed on within the giving circle of God. Goodness, in other words, is meant not to be *had*, but to be *given*.

But how do we give goodness away? The love and beauty behind goodness can be noticed by others. But what will they do when they notice? How will they change?

As I noted in a previous chapter, my kids are "good" at sensing the emotional or spiritual state of others around them. It's like a sixth sense. They pick up on the vibrations of troubled hearts—the murmurs of frustration, the slow beat of sadness, the low violin strum of self-doubt. They hear them. And they respond, often with simple grace: a hug, words of encouragement, refrains of love and value. It's truly beautiful to witness. The beauty lies beneath the goodness, which is given for others in a way that draws something out of us from the depths, bringing it to the light. It brings the inside to the outside, and that is profoundly Christlike. Luke writes that Jesus Christ would be a sign in his times, "so that thoughts from many hearts may be revealed" (Luke 2:35). Jesus would bring the inside (thoughts from many hearts) to the outside (revealed). That, in a related sense, is what beauty does.[10] David Whyte writes,

> Beauty is the harvest of presence, the evanescent moment of seeing or hearing on the outside what already lives far inside us; the eyes, the ears or the imagination suddenly

---

10. This makes perfect sense since the Son is the origin of all beauty. Again, see Hibbs, "Beauty Embodied."

become a bridge between the here and the there, between then and now, between the inside and the outside; beauty is the conversation between what we think is happening outside in the world and what is just about to occur far inside us.[11]

My kids' responses to others draw out other people's inner need for love and kindness in a world that sometimes chills us with cold indifference or pricks us with thorns of criticism. The effect of their beautiful responses is renewed *presence* in the world, a sense of being seen again, valued and cherished as a creature in need of love. Whenever I have the pleasure of watching this happen or experiencing it myself, I say, "Yes, this is good, so very good." Goodness, as with the other fruits of the Spirit, must be given away. It must be held out to others, as the Father does with the Son through the Spirit.

Faithfulness

To be faithful is to stay, to make the tiny choices—morning, midday, and evening. Faithfulness is constant presence on the path marked out for us. This gift, too, is relational to the core and is meant to be given away.

Staying, of course, is buried deep within the Godhead. It's related to the *abiding* of the Son in the Father, and the Father in the Son, and the Spirit in both. Abiding. Dwelling. Faithful presence of persons in persons . . .

And this didn't change with the incarnation. Even

---

11. David Whyte, *Consolations: The Solace, Nourishment, and Underlying Meaning of Everyday Words* (Langley, WA: Many Rivers, 2018), 19.

when the Son stepped into Mediterranean sand, the Spirit (faithfully with him even in the womb of Mary) was faithful. He stayed, and so did the Father. It couldn't be otherwise, for God *is* faithfulness. He's always perfectly present with himself, and that presence is relational; it's a presence of communion.

Faithfulness for us is relational on two levels. First, we are faithful in relationship with the God who beckoned us out of the shadows into the blinding light of his loving holiness. Our faithfulness has him as its primary reference. Are we staying on *his* path?[12] Are we stepping on the stones of fidelity, pressing our feet on the good works he's made for us to walk in (Eph. 2:10)?

> *Are we stepping on the stones of fidelity, pressing our feet on the good works he's made for us to walk in?*

Second is our faithfulness to each other. Do we stay? Are we present and constant when the world shifts beneath the feet of those we love? What about those we hate? What about those toward whom we feel indifferent? Does our faithfulness depend on our feelings? It shouldn't, though it often does.

As I ran through a neighborhood the other day, set with neat and tidy upper middle-class homes—the sort with

---

12. What is this path? It's the path of suffering unto glory, which Paul Miller has called the J-curve. See Paul E. Miller, *J-Curve: Dying and Rising with Jesus in Everyday Life* (Wheaton, IL: Crossway, 2019).

perfect lawns and stone accents on the entryways—the leaves were falling all around me. It's late October as I write, the season when the leaves give up their summer faithfulness and fall to the earth. The change in season calls them to let go, a stern conversation of time and temperature. Bleeding out their beauty in gold and vermillion, they let go of the limbs that held them. Leaves don't stay.

But they do. Come April, they will push out their little blushing bodies in buds. They will appear again. The alleged lack of faith from October will give way to new faithfulness in April.

Of course, these are just leaves. But our faithfulness to others can remind us of the leaves, can't it? We stay faithful in relationships when the weather is fair and the nights are warm. But with the cold from a distant sun—with the adversity or difficulty in upkeep—we wither and fall away.

That's precisely where the gift of the Spirit comes in. He takes the deciduous trees of our faith and makes them conifers. He grows us into evergreens. And the growth happens one tiny choice at a time. It's the Spirit who prods us on in our little moments to stay, to remain.

He takes the deciduous trees of our faith and makes them conifers. He grows us into evergreens.

And if we need a little reminder to push us in the right direction, we can stare at the faithfulness of the Son of God on the cross. It was in the greatest act of faithfulness that he stayed up there, pinned with little shards of metal made by hands *he* had made. When the season of our faithfulness was long into winter, he stayed. He stayed, through ridicule, through searing pain, through shortened breath, through death itself. And, thanks be to God, he stayed through resurrection. The faithfulness of Jesus on that cross is cause for us to stay in whatever relationship seems troublesome or inconvenient to us. He stayed for us when we left him. How can we not stay with others now that he lives in us? We give the gift of faithfulness, we thrive in God's giving circle, simply by being there for others in adversity.

Gentleness

The most powerful man ever to walk the earth was "gentle and lowly of heart" (Matt. 11:29). Dane Ortlund writes, "Meek. Humble. Gentle. Jesus is not trigger-happy. Not harsh, reactionary, easily exasperated. He is the most understanding person in the universe. The posture most natural to him is not a pointed finger but open arms."[13] "Open arms" is a great picture of gentleness. It's a picture of God's willingness to receive and embrace us where we are.[14]

This can come to us in many forms. Gentleness comes in softness of voice, in the quiet nod to another, in the

---

13. Dane Ortlund, *Gentle and Lowly: The Heart of Christ for Sinners and Sufferers* (Wheaton, IL: Crossway, 2020), 19.

14. Note, however, what Tim Keller always says about this: God loves us enough to meet us where we are, but he doesn't leave us where we are. He starts working to make us more like himself, to carry us forward in holiness.

relaxation of muscles. Gentleness never grips; it guides. And it's yet another relational gift to be given away in God's giving circle.

Gentleness never grips; it guides.

It's easy to see how gentleness is a shoot that rises from the deep heart of God, and yet it still amazes me. The infinitely powerful Father, Son, and Spirit are infinitely loving. And gentleness emerges from love. Love is the rich soil that gives gentleness the nutrient it thrives on: *patience.* An infinite God is infinitely patient, because he's infinitely loving, and therefore he's infinitely gentle.

Jesus carried that gentleness around with him. He wore it like a necklace—an ancient heirloom of his Father, its metal purified by the flames of his own Holy Spirit. He wore the necklace everywhere. He never took it off, not even when his own creatures used a different metal to fix his body to a splintered cross. Gentleness hung there, around his neck. This is a cutting reminder for us to listen to the great Word spoken for our ears, a Word that would enter into us and build his house in the soul.

The Spirit gives the same gift to us so that we might resemble Christ and pass along our gentleness to others.

It can be hard to spot the gift of gentleness among ourselves. We're not often looking for it, anyway. We're more fixated on power and beauty and love: the wonderful but often louder gifts. Gentleness is a whisper by comparison.

My youngest, Heidi, is two as I write this. She's still small enough to pick up and set in my lap. When we want to read books, as I did often with each of my kids, I lift her little body gently, as if I were wearing oven mitts. I set her down softly on my left knee. I slide my left arm gently behind her for support. And as I read, I gently turn the pages— softly, gracefully guiding one thing to another: my hands to her torso, my arm to her back, my fingers to the pages. Everything is slow, intentional, and measured. There's only just enough force to complete the movement, no more or less. That's gentleness.

In our attempts to give this gift to others, we must go beyond the physical. We must go into the world of words. We must learn how to *speak* gently. That means, firstly, not speaking at all. Listening is the country from which gentleness emerges. And to listen well requires patience and self-sacrifice. Each moment that we listen, there will be throbbing impulses to interrupt and speak. There will be times when we believe that what we could say is worth more than what we're hearing, or that our words could bring resolve and restoration. But no. We must constantly roll in the drawbridge of the mouth and let our silence speak (for it does). We must continually remind ourselves that it is another soul's turn to express itself. And that means a subtle dying to the self, a cross-carrying habit.[15] For when our hands are full with our own cross, we are ready to be attentive to another, to hold back our hubris in thinking we could be a savior for them if they would just hear our

---

15. As Paul Miller puts it, "Only as we enter into a life of dying to self, of dying love, do we grow deeper in faith." *J-Curve: Dying and Rising with Jesus in Everyday Life* (Wheaton, IL: Crossway, 2019), 85.

words. Listening is the first mark of gentleness. It smooths the ripples in the water so that both people can see their reflections in that moment.

Listening is the country from which gentleness emerges.

Secondly, there comes word-weighing. Word-weighing is steeped in silence. The choosing comes through two principles: *grace* and *truth*. Paul wrote that we are "to speak the truth in love" (Eph. 4:15) and to let our words "give grace to those who hear" (Eph. 4:29). Think of these principles as the thick brush on each side of the path for your tongue. The middle way accounts for the boundary on each side.

The other day, as I went to help my seven-year-old get into the van, it began to rain. Knowing his sensitivity to that, I quickly pressed the button on my keys to open his door. But I didn't see that he had already opened the door for himself. My button pushing closed the door as he was getting in. The edge of the door bumped his head. He was crying and very upset with me. My attempts at apologizing were as powerless as the raindrops hitting the window. He kept repeating to everyone who had ears to hear how mean I was. How would I respond in this little drama?

By God's grace, the Spirit gave me gentleness, though I fumbled it a bit. First came the listening—letting him voice his pain and frustration and fear. It hurt to listen, but I kept my lips closed (I admit to a few eyerolls). Then grace and truth were the hedges beside my tongue. I needed to express the grace first, an open and sincere apology for the accident. That needed repetition, as grace often does. I had to stare at that side of the hedge for a while.

But the truth needed to breathe, too. Calmly and firmly, I told him that I wasn't being mean. It was an accident. I was just trying to help. Grace first, and then truth. With both hedges in view, I let my tongue stride down the middle.

This little episode reminds me that the progression from grace to truth is familiar to the heart of God. God is truth (John 14:6), but he's always acted toward us in grace before re-delivering the clear call to truth. It was while we were still sinners that Christ died for us (Rom. 5:8). Grace led to truth. The two always hold hands in God's mind, but when it comes to us, grace leads. Truth follows. This is the way of gentleness. We have opportunities every day to give it away.

Self-Control

The last gift of the Spirit is perhaps the most amazing, at least to me, for it expresses all the other gifts and is bound up with them. Self-control is like the skin wrapped around the flesh of the other gifts. It holds them together. It protects them. Without self-control, the other gifts become infected and diseased by selfishness.

Self-control makes the hard choices for love, letting our fingers loosen on something so that we can let it go, helping us stand still when we want to chase.

Self-control makes space for joy. It keeps our lesser desires from the room of the soul so that the greater desires can fill the space.

Self-control ushers in peace, slowly, like a quiet child ushering his grandparent into a crowded room. It restrains us and helps us sacrifice what we must for the peace to enter and remain.

Self-control gives forbearance the extra push it needs up the mountain of adversity.

Self-control cuts a path for kindness through the brush of wild self-centeredness.

Self-control shows us again and again what is truly good, what is to be desired above all else.

Self-control is the brother of faithfulness, always making the difficult decision to keep placing one foot in front of the other.

Self-control chooses gentleness over harsh severity, even when the latter is all we want in the moment.

As with all the other gifts of the Spirit, self-control, despite appearances, is primarily relational and must be given for others in God's giving circle.

The "self" of self-control might suggest that this gift is really about us. But self-control is ultimately always about someone else. It's about making a choice that elevates something or someone besides our momentary passions and thoughts, choosing instead something or someone of eternal weight.

The Spirit's gift of self-control was pulsing through the blood of Christ as he marched up the hill with his cross. In a moment, he could have tossed off the cross, straightened his body, and said, "It is finished *now!*" But self-control made the hard choice in each moment to continue on the dusty path and put his Father first. His self-control was for the Father and for us, not for himself.

It's the same for those who walk in Christ's footsteps. Our self-control is for others, for our heavenly Father and for those around us.

One of the hardest places to practice this is diet. This may sound trite to some people, but I find we're often ignorant of how beholden we are to food. For various health reasons, my wife and I switched to a whole-foods, plant-based diet. (This was right for *us*, but I'm not making a plea for all to conform to this.) That continues to demand self-control, especially in a culture that fills the air with the smoke of grilled meat, keeps a thousand dairy products packaged and chilled for our eager fingers, and offers a million "flavor-enhanced" snacks at every grocery store. When I make a decision not to eat something, it feels in that moment as if it's all about me. But it's not. It's about God, who gave me a body as a temple for his worship (1 Cor. 6:19). It's about my wife, who needs me at my best (and being at my best means fueling my body with the things God made for it). It's about my kids, who need to see bodily care modeled, and who could be robbed of their father if he filled his body with unnatural things. Self-control is always about others.

That makes it a bit easier to see how it's a gift that must be given away. Every instance of self-control is a present in the palm of our hands. We lift it up to others. It's not ultimately about us.

Summary

The point in this chapter was to show that the gifts of the Spirit are fundamentally *relational* and are meant to be *given away* for others. That's how the gifts of God work. They are gifts that we receive and then give. That's the giving circle. We can now enhance the diagram from an earlier chapter by drawing in these gifts of the Spirit.

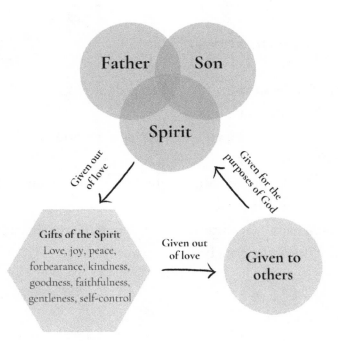

PRAYER

    God, you give so many gifts.
    Your Spirit pours out your character,
    And we stand here holding up

Our empty cups.
Help us to see that the gifts you give
Are meant for others
And are meant for giving.
Help us to focus, one day at a time,
On the gifts you are helping us receive.
And then teach us to give them back
In gratitude.

REFLECTION QUESTIONS

1. Which of the gifts of the Spirit are you most familiar with in your own life?
2. Which of the gifts of the Spirit are you least familiar with in your own life?
3. Which of the gifts of the Spirit is most difficult for you to practice?
4. What is one opportunity you might have this week to give one of these gifts to someone else?

Reader Resource: Charting the Fruit of God

We're repeatedly told throughout Scripture, and by Jesus and Paul, that the fruit of the Spirit should be evident in our lives and that we will "be known" by our fruit (Ezek. 17:23; Dan. 4:12; Matt. 7:15–20; Luke 6:43–45; Gal. 5:16–24). Yet, it can be difficult for us to keep track of our spiritual development. For many of us, we only sometimes ask the questions, "How am I doing spiritually? Where does God want to help me grow and bear more fruit?" We need to be intentional about looking for the fruit of the Spirit (or the absence of it) in our own lives. You can use the table below to start keeping track of the fruit God is growing in your life. This is a chart that should be revisited periodically as you take steps to grow in some areas and remain faithful in others. I've offered an example in the first row.[16]

Fruit of the Spirit	Opportunity for Growth	Reflection on Action
Love	*Show the love of God to your wife by doing something for her without her asking.*	*I made her coffee for her, but I do this regularly. I need to make more of an effort to go out of my way and do something bigger.*
Joy		

---

16. To download this chart for future use, visit http://piercetaylorhibbs.com/the-book-of-giving-reader-resources/.

Fruit of the Spirit	Opportunity for Growth	Reflection on Action
Peace		
Forbearance		
Kindness		
Goodness		
Faithfulness		
Gentleness		
Self-Control		

Chapter 6

For years, I've taught English and writing to non-native and native speakers, and there's a concept called *recycling* in language teaching. It's absolutely critical. You could probably guess its meaning. Recycling is the intentional review of words or skills previously introduced. Recycling is a child of repetition, and repetition is central to all sorts of learning, not just language learning. So, let's do some recycling now before we keep going.

After laying some groundwork for what gifts are, we first gazed at God the Giver and the holy giving circle. We looked at how God gives himself to himself—Father to Son, Son to Father, Spirit to Son; on and on it goes. God is eternally self-giving.

We then looked at how God invites us into his giving circle by breathing his own life into us. This is God's Spirit-gift. Next, we stared in wonder at how the Son of God gave himself to us on the cross. And then we saw how the Spirit of God gives himself to us through spiritual fruit, the topic of the previous chapter.

Pause here with me. Do you see how wildly self-giving God is? Do you see how giving is at the core of his identity?

Do you see how giving is fundamentally circular and how we've been invited into God's giving circle by the creative and redemptive work of the Father, Son, and Spirit? I hope so.

In the next section of the book, we'll focus on gifts more specifically, especially two types: God's gift of creation and God's gift of us to each other. The final section of the book focuses on the need and manner of our daily giving. And then I'll end with a chapter on the constant problems we face as givers.

The Trinitarian Shape of Giving

Before we move on, I want to set out plainly the model of giving we've been discussing because it's so counter-cultural. Giving is not simply an activity, something we do. Rather, it's something *God* does (even something God *is*), and we get the joy of modeling our lives after his. I can't stress this enough, because we're so fixated on giving as *transactional* rather than giving as *circular*. Let me set out the difference.

Transactional giving is linear. It moves from a source, then to a giver, and then to a recipient.

There's nothing particularly wrong with this diagram. It touches on what John Barclay called the principle of *noncircularity*, the idea that gifts are not reciprocated by the receiver; they simply end there, which highlights the generosity of the one who gave.[1] But this is only one facet of giving, and our modern era focuses too much on this. The effect is that we end up with an incomplete picture of giving. Transactional giving acts as if giving stops with the recipient. But we've already seen that the gifts we receive are meant to be given back to others for the purposes of God. That's the giving circle. This is bound with the bedrock truth that "that gifts are a means of creating or sustaining relationships."[2] The giving circle is primarily about *relationships*—God's relationship with us and our relationships with each other.

The Giving Circle

---

1. John Barclay, *Paul and the Power of Grace* (Grand Rapids, MI: William B. Eerdmans, 2020), 32, Kindle edition.

2. Barclay, *Paul and the Power of Grace*, 18, Kindle edition.

The giving circle, we saw, is rooted in God's trinitarian character. The self-giving God has no end to giving. The circle is unbroken.

Now, why does it matter whether we have a transactional or circular approach to giving? Here's the major difference: *The ultimate purpose of our giving shapes both the gift and the act of giving.* In other words, when we're unaware of the purpose for our giving (i.e., to give back to others in praise of the glorious, self-giving God), we may end up giving the wrong gifts for the wrong reasons. This is precisely because we don't have God built into our model of giving.

> *The ultimate purpose of our giving shapes both the gift and the act of giving.*

Let me offer an example. Suppose I want to express love for my wife by making her breakfast. The gift is breakfast. I'm the giver. My wife is the recipient. So, I make her breakfast, she thanks me for it, eats it, and we move on. But what is going on inside *me*, the giver? *Why* did I make her breakfast? There are a few ways in which our sinfulness can breed problems at this point. Here are some of them.

1. I act as if I'm giving out of my own means. In truth, the ultimate giver is God himself. God provided the skills and knowledge I've acquired over the years, which I've used to get a job (which he also provided), which produced money to buy the food. He also gave me a body that's able to make the food and offer it to her. I can't take all the credit for this act of giving because, from the very outset, I'm relying on another, namely God. Ignoring the ultimate giver leads to pride and self-absorption. I walk away from the act of giving thinking *I'm* pretty great rather than worshiping *God* for being a grand giver.

2. My act of giving can contaminate the love-gift I offer. This follows naturally from where we left off. If I think that I'm pretty great as a giver, then I start wanting and expecting acknowledgment. I want credit for the gift I gave. I want my wife, perhaps, to do something to express *my* greatness. Perhaps I even start expecting her to reciprocate this gift somehow. Do you see how this spoils the gift of love that I tried to give? It makes that love-gift ultimately about *me*. And then I start growing impatient. I start carrying a chip on my shoulder. I start to grow envious of the gift (e.g., "I wish someone would make *me* breakfast!"). I also boast to others about the gift I gave (even if that boasting is to myself, on the inside). I become arrogant and rude, insisting that my own righteousness is above reproach, that I'm really a saint in sinner's garb. And then the arrogance bleeds into irritation and resentment. And yet, "Love is patient and kind; love does not envy or boast; it is not arrogant or rude. It does not insist on its own way; it is not irritable or resentful" (1 Cor. 13:4–5). The love-gift I tried to offer is now utterly contaminated. It no longer even resembles love.

3. My experience may make me less likely to give again. All of this makes it far less likely that I'll take the initiative to give again. This is the death of the giving circle. I start focusing on *taking* rather than *giving*. Selfishness replaces selflessness; expectation replaces gratitude. And this grieves the heart of God.

If I ignore the ultimate giver from the outset, everything can easily fall apart. The transactional approach to giving can only ever lead to selfishness. There is no other destination.

Now, let's look at the same act when I use the giving circle. To start, I know that God has lavishly poured out himself for me. He's giving me life and experience and knowledge and relationships. He's given me a wife who loves me deeply and children who find joy in my smile. He's given me *everything* because he's given me himself. In Christ, I possess *all* (2 Cor. 6:10). What more could I ask for?

If God has already given me innumerable gifts, then my act of breakfast making can be pure, by the power of his own Spirit. It can be truly selfless, because I'm not only giving to someone else what God has given to me (moving things along in the giving circle); I'm also not expecting something in return. My hope is only to see my wife's joy. This makes the gift a true act of love.

And people in our world can usually tell the difference between transactional and circular giving. They can sense when giving is done out of a pure heart and when giving is done out of an expectation for reciprocation or praise. It matters. Starting with God in our giving *matters*.

This trinitarian shape of giving—rooted in the Father giving the Son his Spirit without measure (John 3:34)—colors all of our little acts of giving. It takes what seems to be transactional and shows us that the ultimate purpose, for living and for every act we carry out, is God himself. And God's not packing a storehouse full of our gifts. He's not hoarding them. He's always giving. Always.

Do you see the beauty of the giving circle, its eternal continuation? This puts us in a good place to start examining some of the gifts that God has given to us.

PRAYER

> God, you give your Spirit
> To the Son without measure.
> You're always giving.
> And I'm so often taking.
> I receive and hoard.
> I grasp and guard.
> Soften my heart.
> Open my hands.
> Help me this day
> To offer
> What belongs to you anyway.

Reflection Questions

1. How does this trinitarian shape of giving compare with your previous understanding of giving?
2. What are some of the dangers of a transactional approach to giving?
3. What are some of the benefits of a circular approach to giving?

4. What is something that you can receive and then give to someone else this week? Be concrete.

5. What is something you tend to receive but not give?

Reader Resource: The Giving Circle Challenge

The giving circle calls us to pass on what we receive in some way. But we find it very difficult to do this on a regular basis. Choose something you value highly, something you cherish and love. Ask yourself how you might give that thing to someone else. Then offer it and write down what happened. It may well be that things appear to go unchanged. But they have changed. If you don't come to see what has changed, God certainly sees, for he always sees what's done in secret.[3]

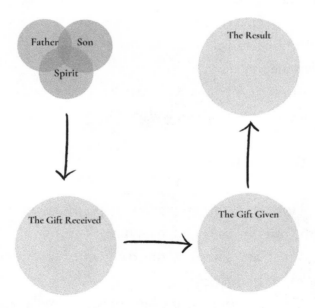

---

3. To download this chart for future use, visit http://piercetaylorhibbs.com/the-book-of-giving-reader-resources/.

Gifts

Chapter 7

N o one is awake yet. The second hand from the clock clicks to keep the quiet rhythm of the morning. Outside, the sun is growing more confident, just above the tree line. Slices of cloud are blushing with pink, and a few ribbons from airplanes still hang frozen in the soft blue.

A few moments later, our house is flooded with light. I couldn't really grasp the moment of transition: it was dark just a few moments ago. And now the living room and kitchen have their shapes and colors and textures given back to them.

The light is a gift to all dark places, giving everything in its radius the name it had before. Light draws out identity.

Light draws out identity.

And I think, "Where did I come from? How did I get here? I came through passion and blood, through silent stirrings in my mother's belly, forming fingernails and follicles, bones and muscle—waiting for the air and then screaming into it.

Here I sit thirty-five years later, holding a pen, drawing

words, looking up at the chalkboard we made for the kids, covered (ironically) in question words.

Creation is a gift we're born into—one great, expansive, ever-moving Christmas morning. And the Giver . . . you know him. Though you have never seen him, deep at the well bottom of your soul, you know he is there. He is here, as you hold this book. He is always *in the room*. He is all around you, for all has come from him, through him, and to him (Rom. 11:36). This is another perspective on the circular nature of God giving, a circle that begins and ends with God.

From

Gift-givers are mysterious. (And why wouldn't they be, if they're drawing on resources from the ultimately mysterious Trinity?) You can never peer into them as you would through water in a glass. You see their smiles, the light in their eyes, the muscles in their cheeks holding back the full revelation. But God has told us what lies behind the face: love (himself). And love, you know by now, is self-giving. Its roots are in the Trinity—the Father loving the Son, and the Son and Spirit loving the Father. This is the holy circle of self-giving from which comes the gift of creation. The *from* of creation, the *from* of *you*, is personal. It's in the person of the Father loving his Son and Spirit. It's in the person of the Son loving his Spirit and Father. It's in the person of the Spirit loving his Father and the Son. Self-giving, tri-personal love is the door to creation.

Self-giving, tri-personal love is the door to creation.

Look at the world around you right now. Your *from* is Father. But so, in a different sense, is the *from* of the tired maple tree outside, and the *from* of the blue jay caught up in its branches, and the *from* of every blade of grass, every turning of the wind, every wisp of cloud, every dog's face.

Your *from* is Son, who made you to utter words in his own image. And so it goes with the *from* of the white oak wood flooring beneath me. The white oak came from the mind of God and was uttered into its barked glory through the eternal Word, who is the Son. As I walk from living room to kitchen, I step on materials that came through the voice of God, the Word.

Your *from* is Spirit. The air in your lungs, the life in your body, the wind-like movements of your limbs as they brush through the atmosphere. So it is with water, as it is shouldered onto the shores by the breeze and the movements of the moon. The repetition, the orbits of the moon, mirror the ever orbiting, self-giving God.

Our *from* finds its origins in divine persons, in the one God.

Through

The gifts of creation all around us have also come *through* God, especially through his Word.[1] It is through the Word

---

1. I've written about this more extensively in *The Speaking Trinity & His Worded World: Why Language Is at the Center of Everything* (Eugene, OR: Wipf & Stock, 2018).

(Heb. 1:2–3; Col. 1:16) that the clock ticks, that the light from my lamp radiates into the room and rakes across the butcher block where I write. It's through the Word that the soft piano notes wander into the room from the tiny speakers in my phone. It's through the Word that my children's bodies lay sleeping in their beds, taking in every momentary gift of oxygen as the neurons in their brains join hands and sing dreams into shape.

The writer of Hebrews says that all things are held together by the word of the Word's power (Heb. 1:3). That means every gift of creation is, when you think about, beautifully fragile. The Son of God could utter a syllable and bring an end to the *through*, to the holding together. That, I think, is precisely what happens when something in our world ends. When a leaf curves in on itself and lets go of the limb that sent it life, the Word has said, "The through is finished."

It's different with persons. When my father's soul left our living room in my childhood home, the Word said, "Through is finished. Come, enter the forever." For my father had wings to get to eternity, and wind from the Spirit to lift him up.

We don't think often enough about this beautiful fragility of life, how everything at this very moment is hooked and held together by divine speech. One sovereign syllable would make an end of it all.

Instead, things end more like the autumn leaves outside: letting go in symphonies, dropping away in harmonious refrains, like lines in a song that are overlapping, some going on and others going out—all at the perfect and punctuated will of God. This is our beautifully fragile world. The *through* of all things rests on God's tongue.

The through of all things rests on God's tongue.

To

And what's the point of it all? Him. A person is the destination of all things. He's the purpose. Every gift of creation, from hair follicles to human souls, is given so that it can be given *back*. Do you see the circularity, mirroring the circularity of God's eternal self-giving? The thought is puzzling at first but grows glorious with meditation.

All gifts have a purpose and end. All gifts have a *to*. The notebook I'm writing in now was a gift from my wife, a birthday present. Its purpose, its end, is to be filled with words. I fill the notebook with words so that I can give them to you, who are kind enough to bless *me* by picking up this book. The gift was given so that it might be regifted. Its *to* is for others. Its purpose is persons. And the greatest person will receive the glory and love and passion and honor of every gift, the person of the Son. All things are not just *from* him and *through* him, but *to* him. There could be no greater recipient for every gift given in creation. In fact, the one to whom all gifts are given is the one who knows their value and purpose beyond our understanding. Gifts are not lost when they go to him; they are found. They realize their glorious end by shining more light on the beauty of *his* self-giving.

Herein lies the great mystery of gift giving. *Gifts are given so that they might be given back.* This is the giving circle. *For* him, *through* him, and *to* him . . . who could have ever imagined?

PRAYER

God, thank you for your Son,
That ancient Word,
From whom,
Through whom,
And to whom are all things.
Thank you that all things given
Are accepted through him
And are sent back to him.

Thank you that your Son
Is freely given,
Freely received,
And freely proclaimed
In the power of the Holy Ghost.

REFLECTION QUESTIONS

1.   In what ways does viewing creation as coming from the Son differ from viewing creation as an impersonal evolutionary process?

2.   How does the truth that all things come through the Son help you worship God and appreciate your surroundings?[2]

3.   If all things are meant to go to the Son, serving his purposes, what does that mean for things that seem to go against God's redeeming work?

4.   How can you pray for someone who is struggling with the to aspect of reality—the ultimate purpose for all things? Write down your prayer and pass it on to that person.

Reader Resource: from, through, and to

We mirror God in all the good things we do. We can't help but imitate. Life is mimesis. So, as all things are from,

---

2. For examples of perceiving God in the world around you, see *Finding God in the Ordinary* (Eugene, OR: Wipf & Stock, 2018); and Joel Clarkson, *Sensing God: Experiencing the Divine in Nature, Food, Music, and Beauty* (Carol Stream, IL: NavPress, 2021).

through, and to the Son, we also have gifts that flow from us, through us, and to us. Think of one gift you can give this week that will come from you, one that will come through you, and one that will come to you from another. For each gift, consider how the Son of God is the ultimate from, through, and to. An example is provided in the first row.[3]

Direction	Example	Relation to the Son
From	*I was asked to write a foreword to a friend's book, so that will be a gift from me to the author.*	*The Son has written the foreword to my salvation and redemption. He has penned words on my heart that foreshadow my story and its ending. He has read my life like a book and knows exactly what to say about it.*
From		
Through		
To		

---

3. To download this chart for future use, visit http://piercetaylorhibbs.com/the-book-of-giving-reader-resources/.

Chapter 8

I sit here in the morning dark, covered with gifts. The t-shirt I'm wearing was a birthday gift from my younger brother. It has a picture of Laketown on it, from *The Hobbit*. The watch on my left wrist, along with my jeans and socks, were things I purchased with money God gave to me, through my work. My glasses, as well, came from money that God gave.

And it's not taken lightly that I *can* work. Not only do I have a job, but I have a mind that allows me to do it—a mind that has wandered through a bachelor's degree, and then three master's degrees. How many ideas scudded through the expanse of my blue mind (most of which are not understood or appreciated)? How many attempts to express on the outside what was on the inside? How many gifts of time—moments, minutes, months—rolled right in front of me? And how many poor decisions, foolish decisions, selfish decisions, that might have turned out for my harm (even my death), but didn't?

I'm still here. I'm still bathing in the gifts of my prodigal God. And as I write these words for you, I ask, "What do we do with the gifts we've been given? What do we *do* with them?" There's a *descriptive* and *prescriptive* answer to that question. If you've made it this far in the book, you know the prescriptive answer: we're supposed to use the gifts we receive to give to others, continuing the arc of God's giving circle.

But the descriptive answer is short and sad: We open them and move on. We don't pause to thank the Giver. We don't wait for intentionality. We just keep tearing through the wrapping paper, second by second, thing by thing, beauty by beauty.

I'm not naive. I know we can't voice a "thank you" every second of the day. We'd never be able to do anything else. Perhaps, though, we could go with a mind shift. We could pick up our soul and turn it around so that it's facing the light of gratitude. It might even start as we wake and utter words that point us in the right direction.

> God, you give. And I receive.
> My hands are open, and my heart.
> Give me the grace I need to believe
> That you've been giving from the start.

But what we do with gifts goes beyond a pair of couplets.

We do with our gifts what we do with everything else: we follow God, his broad and beautiful back. And we've already seen that God is eternally self-giving, and that gifts are given so that they might be given back.

It's no coincidence, for me, that I'm marking the pages of my notebook, penning out the first draft of this book, as Christmas approaches like a tired and happy grandfather strolling slowly through autumn.

"Christmas is the season of giving," we hear. And yet we have so little understanding of what that means.

The season of giving, like a speck of dust in a sun-soaked room, is enveloped by the atmosphere of the God who gave *himself* . . . all of it. He didn't give a mere gift; he gave *himself*. Sit here for a few moments with that sentence.

He didn't give a mere gift; he gave himself.

God, you see, belongs to himself. He owes nothing to anyone; he's fully self-sufficient, fully personal. He's the only being like that. There is no necessary pull within God to rely on another. He's a diamond spinning in a sun room, reflecting the rainbow of his own reality off the walls.

We, on the other hand, "live under the burden and illusion of self-ownership."[1] We carry around the lie that *we* are self-sufficient and independent—and thus anyone who receives a gift from us should truly count his blessings, for we left our royal self-sufficiency to give something of our resources to another.

The truth is that we're already possessed. We're already fully reliant on another. Any gift that we give is also a gift of God, for all that we possess—in our personhood, resources, and thoughts—is *his* possession. We *can't* give on our own.

Do you see the vast difference between us and God? This beautiful, loving, three-personed Lord—King of

---

1. Kelly M. Kapic, *The God Who Gives: How the Trinity Shapes the Christian Story* (Grand Rapids, MI: Zondervan, 2018), 19, Kindle edition.

silence and starlight—gave not just all we see around us, but himself. That's why Christmas is truly magical. How could God give so much? How could God possibly give that *kind* of gift? How could he wrap the Son in sinews and skin and push him into the loud and careless world?

And not only that. It was a gift for Christ to *live* among us, but Christ *gave* his life away for us. Every bead of sweat, every skin scratch from a stone, every perception of the eyes, every word from his mouth, every movement of his legs and hands—each grain of his existence was placed into a sack and handed to *us*. Are you starting to feel the weight of that gift?

Now, what are we to do with that Christmas gift, the gift of God himself? We must remember always what Kelly Kapic calls "the movement of divine generosity." This is a new way of saying what we've already been rehearsing in this book: God gives his gifts so that they might be given back. "The Scriptures present the movement of divine giving and receiving as a cycle: everything comes from God, is sustained through him, and will be given back to him."[2]

We've talked about how counterintuitive this is, so we need to revisit it once more. Gifts can't truly be gifts if we give them back, can they?

Well, it all goes back to our understanding of *possession*. What does it mean to *have* something? For some of us, possession means keeping something to ourselves, calling it "ours" and not someone else's. The Bible I read each morning is *mine*, not another's.

---

2. Kapic, *The God Who Gives*, 19, Kindle edition.

But that way of thinking leaves out two very important truths: (1) we don't ever have full control of things in the world; and (2) we are going to have to leave the world eventually. To whom will my Bible belong when I die? My wife and kids, I hope. What was mine will be theirs. Ownership flows on like a river, passing from person to person. The gifts we receive are not eternal ice blocks that we hoard in the cold. They seem like ice at first. But then they melt. They reduce and drip through the cracks between our fingers. We have some control over where the water lands. But God is the real controller, taking the water where it needs to go next.

Ownership flows on like a river, passing from person to person.

Jessica Hiatt, a gifted artist who has designed many of my book covers, designed the image below as an initial idea for the cover. Though we ultimately went with something else, I still find this image to be a beautiful representation of how gifts truly work in our world.

The water goes from hand to hand. Eventually it all goes back to God, who uses every gift for his own good purposes. "All things are from him, through him, and to him," remember?

My point is that giving gifts back (to others and to God) doesn't do anything to invalidate the gift. Recall that in Barclay's "perfections" of a gift, *noncircularity* is only one facet. And we get too hung up on that. Gifts aren't ultimately meant to be possessed; they're meant to be passed on. They're meant to create, sustain, and develop *relationships*. That's the beauty of divine generosity spilling into our waiting palms.

Do you possess the gifts you've been given, or do you look for ways to give them back? Holy Spirit, help us all to move the water on to other hands.

PRAYER

> Lord, we don't understand possession.
> We think we own,
> When you own.
> We think we have,
> When you have lent.
> Teach our hearts to see
> That you are the one
> Who holds all things.
> You are the rich one.

We are the needy.
Help us to find lasting joy
In your generosity.

REFLECTION QUESTIONS

1. What areas of your life seem to call for more gratitude?
2. What things do you cling to most as your possessions?
3. "Ownership flows on like a river, passing from person to person." What things do you most long to pass on to others?
4. How does viewing gifts as "water," passing from one hand to another, change the way you receive them?

Reader Resource: Seeing the Water of Giving

Intentionality, for me, is a hallmark of learning and spiritual growth. We have to be intentional about what we think and how we act if we're going to change. One place to start is to *notice* where the water of giving has already been. Think of a gift that has come to you from God. Then pray about how that gift can be passed on to someone else.[3]

---

3. To download this chart for future use, visit http://piercetaylorhibbs.com/the-book-of-giving-reader-resources/.

Giving

Chapter 9

We have learned much about God as Giver, about the gifts he gives, and what we're to do with them. The central thought for this book has been repeated frequently: **Giving is circular, and God makes us givers by drawing us into his giving circle.** Now comes the time to focus on practice. This final section is a call for us to unclench our fists, unfurl our fingers, and give. How do we do that on a daily basis? That's where we're headed.

But I'll tell you at the outset that the recommendations I offer in the chapters ahead are areas in which I need to grow much. I write these words for myself, in hopes that I'll become the type of daily giver God wants me to be. I walk *with* you in these pages, not ahead of you.

In this chapter, we'll focus on the gift of *time*. That seems to be the broadest gift we can give, and so we'll move from this to more specific types.

Time is often linked metaphorically to water, and for good reason. Water thrives in movement, coursing around us, carrying us in its current, never looking back. That's why it's so precious. We can't cup it or control it. We can only swim in it, looking backwards and forwards as we bob in the present. Even in this undulating expanse, we grip the illusion of ownership, of sole possession. But time is as good a teacher as it is a mystery. As we pass through it, we say, "Oh . . . so that's what time is. I can't go back. I can't hold it."

So, how can we possibly give this thing we can't hold? It's all a matter of *focus in stewardship*. As we wake in the morning, the seconds drifting through the dark, we can choose where we look and for how long. As I write this morning, my focus is on the page as my pen marks the paper. I'm giving time (the time given to me) to a task that I hope and pray will be a blessing to *you*. This is my focus. And because I don't own this time I sit in, it's a matter of stewardship, of directing what God has given in the ways he's directed in his word. Focus in stewardship.

The act of focusing is a great gift in a world full of competing voices and a million distractions. In our world, to focus is to hold up a magnifying glass against a tiny thing— to stare and work and marvel.

All of this still sounds abstract, so here are some practical applications to consider.

1. Focus your attention on someone as they speak. Listening is an art, not a chore. And it's an artform slipping away from us in a crazed culture where everyone believes he's a fountain of truth that the dehydrated masses need to drink from. I know I've talked about listening already, but it needs repeating. It's *so* lost on us.

Listening is an art, not a chore.

Listening is a great gift of time because it takes who and where we are and offers them to another who wants or needs to be seen and heard.

I have a hard time with this because I can be very task oriented. There's always a churning drive in me to get things done, and that can make me feel like I'm always balancing on a pinhead while I'm trying to listen to someone.

Having a seven-year-old, five-year-old, and two-year-old right now—a truly precious era in the little stream of my own life—means I'm always called on to listen, to see the latest paper-and-tape construction, to hear what happened in the most recent *Geronimo Stilton* book, to soak in the words of an animated stuffed bear. It can be easy to pass these things off as not truly important, but that is a mistake. For my kids, these things make their little hearts beat faster. They open the storehouses of wonder and imagination inside them. They illuminate the hours.

In the bustle of breakfast cleanup, it's a gift of love to put down the dishes, dry off my hands, and stare into my kids' eyes, blazing with life. "What? What did your bear say?" It's just as important and generous to do this for a toddler as it is for a state senator. Listening is a gift that cups our time and hands it to someone else, if only for a moment. Such moments are gold.

2. Focus on the task at hand. Again, our generation is plagued by distraction. Blaise Pascal said long ago that nothing was so hard for a man as to sit in a room by himself. How much harder it has become for us! Just to focus on what we're doing at the moment is a gift. But to whom is it given? It all depends.

Focusing on washing the dishes is a gift to my family. Focusing on writing an email is a gift to the recipient. Focusing on raking the leaves—really watching them lift and gather and float—is a gift to God, showing that the time he has given us is examined and measured and noticed.

In all this, we forget that distraction can be a form of an insult. Distraction says, "I will not commit to giving all of myself to this."

I'll be the first to admit my hourly failure with this. Focus is a practice. It must be cultivated and cared for like a farmer's field. The longer we let it lie fallow, the more the weeds and saplings rebel and consume the soil.

3. Focus on your soul development. We spend so little time reflecting on the hard and heavy work God is doing on us. He's ever shaping and scraping and sanding. He's modeling us to the image of his Son. Right now.

I've come to be bothered by a certain question— whether asked of me or of someone else when no answer is forthcoming. "How are you being shaped to Christ right now?" See, this is the most important thing that could happen to a human being: that you could be made more like the Son of God (Rom. 8:29)! How wild and mysterious is that?

And yet we don't pray earnestly and search in God's word for the catalysts of that shaping. We're often completely ignorant of how our soul is changing and developing. Or even of how it *could* change, how it *needs* to change.

Finding daily time to pray over and reflect on the status

of your soul is first a gift to God, who is constantly at work, and second a gift to others, who will be the recipients of God's soul work in you, and of your mindfulness to it.

I'll give you an example. Lately, God has been showing me how selfish I can be—putting little needs or wants that I have before the wants and needs of my family. I make my breakfast first. I get a glass of water for myself first. I prepare my coffee before my wife's. I find something to eat or something to put away before I listen to my kids tell me about their latest Lego creation.

Finding little pockets of the day to put my wife and kids first is an intentional acknowledgement of my soul development (and I fail daily). It's an acknowledgement that Christ lived an others-first life. He gave up all and kept nothing for himself. I want to be like my elder brother (Heb. 2:11–12). I want to live like that. And the maturing change won't happen as one major momentous event. It will happen in coffee brewing, in looking at Legos, in making someone a piece of toast.

Focusing on your soul development is a great gift to God and others. It's a beautiful gift of time, handing off what we hold as God shapes us to his Son.

PRAYER

> God, we think that time is ours.
> We think of time as a thing to hold,
> When it's running gold,
> Flowing all around us,

Drifting to the currents you set.
Rather than trying to grip the current,
We ask that you help us find little ways
To give our time to others.
In this, let us image you,
Who created time
And then gave it away
To save your people.

REFLECTION QUESTIONS

1.   To whom could you give the gift of focused listening this week?
2.   What tasks this week would be good to offer to God and others as you focus intensely on them?
3.   What's an area of soul development that you can pray over this week? Try to set a small goal for change.
4.   In what other ways can you give your time to others?

Reader Resource: Time-Giving Log

It's not practical to log our gifts of time in a journal. But it can be beneficial to choose one type of giving and track our behavior for a week or so. This shows us how willing we are to give and where we need to pray for more help from the Spirit. Choose a particular means of giving your time. Note each day how you did with this sort of giving by answering the question provided. How would you like to pray for change? What work of the Spirit can you rejoice in already? I've offered an example in the first row.[1]

Day	Question	Response/Notes
E.g.	What (if anything) got in the way of your giving?	*Tasks. I really felt pulled to finish cleaning up the kitchen before listening to one of my kids describe what they had made for me (an activity book).*
1	What (if anything) got in the way of your giving?	
2	How did the recipient respond to your gift?	
3	What did you feel or think after giving the gift?	
4	Did anyone else notice you giving the gift?	
5	When is giving this gift most difficult for you?	

---

1. To download this chart for future use, visit http://piercetaylorhibbs.com/the-book-of-giving-reader-resources/.

Day	Question	Response/Notes
6	What can you pray for after giving the gift?	
7	When will you have an opportunity to give the gift again?	

Chapter 10

G iving words is our focus for this chapter. Words are grace-gifts. They open doors and windows in the soul, calling in light to clear the doubt and dread, the fears and failures, the insults and insecurities. As the Word is the light of men (John 1:14), our words are meant to be lights for men, reflecting the self-sacrifice, grace, and hope that comes from his person and work. Is that how you give words? Is that how I give them?

> ## *As the Word is the light* of *men (John 1:14), our words are meant to be lights* for *men.*

Giving words as gifts points out a striking application of the giving circle. It shows how words have the power to push others toward God. To me, this makes perfect sense, since I define language as *communion behavior*, something we do in order to draw closer to another.[1]

---

1. For a short introduction to this idea, see the article "What Is Language? Communion Behavior," http://piercetaylorhibbs.com/what-is-language-communion-behavior/.

God gave his Word (the Son) to us in the power of his Spirit. Why? To draw us closer to himself. When Paul talks about having our words "give grace to those who hear" them (Eph. 4:29), he's echoing the song of the gospel. He's calling us to use words to push others closer to God.

But what does this look like, and how can we know that we've done it? Let me give an example of some words my father wrote to me when I was eight, before his first major brain surgery, when it looked as if he was about to leave the world. Here's how he ended the letter.

> You are never really alone. This is true, not a wish.

The first sentence restates a clear biblical truth. The second confronts a typical response. Combined, they give me grace. Let me unpack this.

While it's true that I'm never really alone because God is always with me, my dad seemed to be talking about *his* presence with me. Just before this, he had written, "My love is as close as a prayer, sweetheart." He wanted me to know that *he* was with me somehow. Is that possible?

The moment my father died, ten years after he wrote that letter, his soul flew to Christ like a song sparrow. He met the bright and burning embrace of his heavenly Father, leaning on the Son and wrapped in the shawl of the Holy Ghost. There he is. He's more alive now than I can imagine. And if Christ himself, with the Spirit, is still praying for me (Rom. 8:34; Heb. 7:25), is it so far of a leap to say that my father is praying for me, too? We have a pattern of following Christ wherever he goes. Why would my dad not follow him on a path of prayer?

So, I believe that my father is praying for me, and in that sense he is *with* me—for the words of creatures are patterned after the words of their Creator, and the Creator's words evoke his presence.[2] There is a mysterious sense in which my father is with me through his words.

And the second sentence reveals a typical response to that idea: doubt. "My dad isn't really with me; he's dead. We're separated, and there's no comfort for me now. This was just my dad's wishful thinking."

And so he wrote, "This is true, not a wish." Truth is so bright that we mistake it for the sun, for something more

---

2. See John M. Frame, *Doctrine of the Word of God*, A Theology of Lordship (Phillipsburg, NJ: P&R, 2010) and Vern S. Poythress, *In the Beginning Was the Word: Language—A God-Centered Approach* (Wheaton, IL: Crossway, 2009).

tangible, something we can hold with our eyes. But real truth goes beyond holding, beyond the blinding sun. Real truth holds *us*. It's so big and broad that we can't see all of it. And we let that mislead us into thinking it's not there, that it couldn't be. And that's why we need the truth repeated so frequently. Again and again, it must enter our ear canals and drift along the streams that feed the heart, introducing and re-introducing the hope that comes from someplace outside of this world.

That's why he wrote, "This is true, not a wish." And I keep reading those words every day, since I've framed his letter above my desk.

But how do these words give me grace? How are they grace-gifts? Grace, I've learned, is receiving what you don't deserve. But what is the "what"? What does grace actually give? Many things, of course, but all of them are bound to love and hope. And love and hope are bound ultimately to the God who *is* love, the God who painted hope across the horizon line of humanity.

Real truth goes beyond holding, beyond the blinding sun. Real truth holds us.

My father's words give grace because they point me to his love and the hope of seeing him again. But that love and hope are groundless on their own. They can only be true of *God*, who *is* love and holds out eternal hope to us. And because they are true of him, my father's words can cling to that truth and echo through my own life.

At their best, our words can be grace-gifts whenever they draw others toward the love and hope housed in the Trinity.

Words are precious, reader, for they resonate deep in the heart of God, who gave the eternal Word to us in love, for our hope. Let us give words to others in his Spirit.

PRAYER

> God of love and hope,
> You have given us the best Word.
> We pause now to hear it.
> Christ. Christ. Christ.
> What a word . . .
> He gives grace beyond measure
> And love unrestrained.
> Help us to follow him
> By giving words that give grace.
> Let the letters and syllables we speak
> Lift others closer to the light
> That is you,
> That light beyond all lights,
> Burning, healing, welcoming.

REFLECTION QUESTIONS

1. What challenges do you face in offering words to others as grace gifts?
2. Identify someone in your life who needs to hear uplifting words. Write out a prayer for that person.

3. How have the grace gifts of others been a blessing to you? Think of a particular example.

4. If our words can give grace to those who hear, what else can they do, on the opposite end of the spectrum?

Reader Resource: Words of Love and Hope

It's so easy to speak words of love and hope to others, to give grace to them, and yet many of us have a hard time doing this. But when the Spirit prompts us and we follow through, we see the effect, and it's beautiful. Use the table below to write down one message of love and hope for someone in your life, and then find a way to deliver the message. Note the response, if you're able.[3]

Words of Love and Hope	Response

---

3. To download this chart for future use, visit http://piercetaylorhibbs.com/the-book-of-giving-reader-resources/.

Chapter 11

Giving *actions* will be the focus of this chapter. Giving actions, compared with giving words, is sort of like the difference between a song with lyrics and an instrumental. Both are beautiful, and sometimes one is more fitting for the occasion than the other.

I took an afternoon run the other week—late November. I had headphones in with some music to keep me motivated, to keep my spirit strong as I came up some of those rolling hills in the Pennsylvania countryside.

Fifty yards ahead, I saw newspaper ads blowing on the shoulder of the road. That's not so common in a rural area with pristine homes and well-kept lawns. It stuck out like a coarse word on a quiet landscape.

On the other side of the road, an old man was trying to gather pieces of the paper as they drifted in the wind. I jogged passed a few of them and felt the Spirit's prompting: "Bend down and pick them up. What are you waiting for? He's watching you. Are you indifferent to the world?"

I reached down every few steps and grabbed a page, crumpling it in my fist. As I came parallel with the old man, he smiled and waved. I did the same, and then grabbed a few more and kept moving. I carried them with me for the last mile of my run and threw them into our own garbage can when I got home. The whole episode made me feel closer to humanity. It reminded me that strangers can still be fellow gardeners in the world. We're not so isolated.

It was a wordless gift, the sort I need to give much more often. It was a gift of action. And I was happy it was just the two of us, strolling down the blustery streets, picking up paper mistakes. Of course, it would've been better if no one else were there.

Giving actions can be the most challenging sort of gift, for it calls us to movement, and we're prone to inertia. We're also, as John Calvin would say, curved in on ourselves (*incurvatus in se*). Our souls default to the letter C. We're often looking to our own needs and wants before we're even aware of the needs and wants of others. When that sad truth is combined with inertia, the gift of action for others seems impossible.

> *Giving actions can be the most challenging sort of gift, for it calls us to movement, and we're prone to inertia.*

That's why we're so struck by Jesus. Jesus did everything for others—prayed, preached, healed, taught, rebuked, even died. And that tells us much about God, for Jesus was both the son of man and Son of God. Since we know God is a giver by nature, the beauty of Christ's self-giving life is felicitous with the heart of God. Gifts of action for others reflect who God *is*, not just who we aim *to be*.

We can feel this in our souls when we hear of someone volunteering at a soup kitchen or children's hospital. I felt it when I saw the old man picking up newspaper scraps. Action for others illuminates the world with the ancient glow of God's own nature.

PRAYER

> God, we're prone to sit,
> To stare at ourselves.
> Acting is not easy.
> And yet you always act
> On our behalf.
> You always work for us and in us.
> Spirit, straighten our backs
> So that we can look around us
> And move in the world
> For grace.

REFLECTION QUESTIONS

1. What's a time when you gave a gift of action? Describe the effect it had, if it was noticed.
2. What sorts of action-gifts are you able to give on a regular basis?
3. What action-gifts do you really not want to give? What seems to hold you back?

4. What action-gifts of Jesus are most striking to you? Why?

Reader Resource: The GIFT Acronym

Giving action-gifts to others and to God needs to be routine. Mnemonic devices have always been helpful for me in turning intentions into habits. The acronym below may help you choose at least one type of action-gift to carry out each day.

G	*Go out of your way.* Do something for someone else that requires you to be inefficient in a task for yourself.
I	*Incur a cost.* Do something for someone else that costs you money.
F	*Find a resource.* Find something that will help someone else solve a problem or address an issue. Then deliver it.
T	*Treat someone.* Give something savory to someone else (i.e., a special coffee, food, or anything else that appeals to the senses).

Chapter 12

In this chapter, we focus on giving *money*. Money is an interesting gift. It's a symbol of sacrifice—either yours or someone else's. And in our world, it's a symbol that unlocks many doors. That's why it so easily becomes an idol.

I once heard of a famous actor who was asked about what it was like to be so wealthy. His answer was illuminating. He said he wished everyone could have wealth and fame because then they would see that it isn't the answer. Money doesn't solve every problem that we imagine it would.

Do you know why? We can only be satisfied by what or whom we are made for. We are made for God. Our puzzle-piece of a soul only matches perfectly with the jigsaw of God. Money will never do all we think it can. That's why the best use of money is giving it away.

Our puzzle-piece of a soul only matches perfectly with the jigsaw of God.

Yet money does reveal quite a bit about our soul. This was always brought home to me by the story of the poor widow.

⁴¹ And he sat down opposite the treasury and watched the people putting money into the offering box. Many rich people put in large sums. ⁴² And a poor widow came and put in two small copper coins, which make a penny. ⁴³ And he called his disciples to him and said to them, "Truly, I say to you, this poor widow has put in more than all those who are contributing to the offering box. ⁴⁴ For they all contributed out of their abundance, but she out of her poverty has put in everything she had, all she had to live on." (Mark 12:41–44)

After reading this several times, I wrote in the margins of my Bible, "Giving is a ratio of the heart." Jesus, as he so often does, cuts through the fog of appearances. It looks as if all the wealthy people in the temple are giving *more*, but he points out that they're giving *less*. Why? Giving is a ratio of the heart, not a simple numeric. Put differently, it's not so much *what* you give; it's what you give *out of.* This widow gave out of her poverty. She had little, and yet she gave much. The others gave out of their wealth. They had much, and yet they gave little. Do you see the heart ratio? This is pivotal for us to understand (and to keep understanding). What you do with your money reveals what you do with your heart. The heart is the treasure house of the soul. What you store there reveals what you truly value.

Giving is a ratio of the heart.

Giving money away also lets you keep more in your heart. Jesus said that the heart resides with its treasure (Matt. 6:21;

Luke 12:34). The less money you keep close to your heart, the more space there will be to fill it with God's passions and purposes. Give away money, and the treasure of God grows greater. Covet it, and the treasure of God appears to shrink.

Giving money to others—be it persons, charities, or organizations—is a gift of sacrifice. It offers what is precious to you (or at least precious in the world) to someone else so that another person might do more. And, we hope and pray, that doing more means giving more to others. And so the circle of giving rolls onward. We give in the hope that giving goes on.

One of my earlier memories was being on vacation with my family in Cape Cod, Massachusetts, strolling the aisles of a craft show with my parents and brothers. I was about ten years old. Back then, we were each given spending money for the vacation. I usually burned through all of it in a few days. But this year I hadn't. Something moved in me as I walked in the warm sunshine that flooded the tablecloth displays of ornaments and jewelry.

And then I saw it: a little glass guitar. A glassworker hung dozens of little ornaments from a wooden rack, made from every color you could imagine. Most of the ornaments were trimmed with brass. I remember that little guitar so well, made from yellow, black, and white glass. It was ten dollars. That was a lot of money back then, for a ten-year-old. I handed over my ten-dollar bill and bought the guitar, which was then wrapped in white tissue paper and handed to me in a brown paper bag.

I had bought it for my dad, who played the guitar and led worship in our church. He loved to play, so I thought of him as soon as I saw the little yellow guitar dangling from a piece of fishing line. It seemed to capture his love so simply.

I gave it to him a few minutes later, and I still remember his surprise and gratitude. That was a moment I will never forget. I was—and am—so prone to selfishness that the whole experience rose above my selfishness like a rose among thorns. Somehow by the prompting and power of God's own Spirit, I had taken a ten-dollar symbol of sacrifice and given it away for someone else. And after the initial sting of being out ten dollars, I felt more open to the world and to the God who governed it; I felt lighter, more moveable.

Giving *lightens* us. That's why Jesus asked those who were heavy laden to come to him and take up his yoke (Matt. 11:28–30). Jesus is a giver by nature (since he is God, and God is a giver by nature). His burden was light because he was always giving, and he was calling us to do the same. But it wasn't just an act of following he wanted. Jesus isn't merely a moral example. He is life itself, and when he called us to be *in* him (John 17), he was calling us to enter the life of the Giver. The life-giving Spirit (1 Cor. 15:45) is the one responsible for our giving. Jesus was calling us to *himself*, but he was also calling us into the giving circle, where he knew the Spirit would help us stretch out our fingers.

Giving, my friend, lightens the soul because it aligns us with the one who controls all things, with the one who constantly gives himself away in order to make more givers in his own image. Giving money is simply one more way to conform to the Giver, to grow lighter, to witness the divine dance of generosity.

PRAYER

> God, we cling to money.
> Our knuckles are white.
> We don't want to loosen our grip.
> But we know it's temporary
> And that its value is so limited
> In comparison with who you are,
> With what you give.
> Help us to be more like the widow,
> Whose heart-ratio showed
> Where her treasure was,
> Where her hope and faith lived.
> Help us to give out of our poverty.
> And as we do this,
> Ignite our joy in you,
> Our eternal treasure.

REFLECTION QUESTIONS

1. Describe a time when you gave money to someone else. What did the experience teach you?
2. When are you most tempted to cling to money? What's the effect of that clinging?
3. If giving is a ratio of the heart, what does that say

about the sorts of money gifts you have offered in your life so far?

4. Giving money can lighten the soul, but that also means coveting money can weigh it down. When do you feel weighed down by coveting money? What does that weight make you long for?

Reader Resource: The Heart Ratio

You can use the diagram below to assess the giving you carry out regularly. What does the heart ratio tell you about where your treasure lies with a particular act of giving? The idea is that you form a habit in giving out of your poverty rather than out of your abundance, though the latter is also a blessing to others.

The Heart Ratio

Conclusion: Giving as Self-Sacrifice

We have now learned about God as Giver, about his giving circle, and about the myriad gifts he gives. We've looked at what their purpose is and seen some of the ways we can give ourselves to others. By staring at God's giving circle, we've noticed that all we are given is given back.

As we reach the end of our time together, there is one basic truth I'd like to leave you with. Since I started the book by laying some groundwork about what a gift is, it seems appropriate to end there as well. But I'll use different language than John Barclay used in describing the "perfections" of gifts.

It seems evident that *giving is self-sacrifice*. B. B. Warfield once wrote of Christ, "He was led by His love for others into the world, to forget Himself in the needs of others, to sacrifice self once for all upon the altar of sympathy."[1] Beautiful words, aren't they?

Jesus is and will always be the greatest gift, given by our Father, ushered to the earth in the warmth and power of

---

1. Quoted in Paul E. Miller, *J-Curve: Dying and Rising with Jesus in Everyday Life* (Wheaton, IL: Crossway, 2019), 148, Kindle edition.

the Holy Spirit. How did he handle himself? His love led him to forget himself, *to give himself away* for others, and all on the altar of *sympathy*. He saw us. The Son of God looked through the haze of our sin and selfishness and saw *us*. He saw our worth in his Father's eyes. He saw our needs. He saw our brokenness. And he gave himself.

How are you going to respond now that this book is drawing to a close? I hope that the answer is to look for ways to give yourself to others. Our God is a Giver. And we are made in his giving image. So, let us give within God's giving circle. Let us give until we have nothing left. For it is then, Christ tells us through the words of Paul, that we will possess everything (2 Cor. 6:10).

The Giver

Father, Son, and Spirit, each to each,
God is a Giver well beyond reach.
But he gave himself below
So that we might hold and know
The truth that giving lends
Ourselves to others' ends,
And calls us to adore
The God who gives much more
Than we could ever seek.

Appendix 1: Suffering and Giving

I didn't plan on writing this book. In the books I'd written up to this point, I'd been ministering to readers who struggled with anxiety and hardship.[1] And then a book on giving? Why?

It's come home to me that giving is often the fruit of hardship. That was one of the main themes in Finding Hope in Hard Things. Through the hard things that we face, God shapes us into givers, for that's what he is. There is a relationship—though we want to deny it in our spirit—between suffering and giving. Let me unpack this a bit.

When things are going well for us, it's certainly possible to give. Nothing is holding us back . . . except the inner desire to *stay* well. Think of your own experiences for a moment. Recall something good that's happened to you lately. It could be receiving a gift from someone else, or having success at work, or enjoying the deep acceptance of another person whom you love. Do you have something in mind?

Now, ask yourself this question: *What changed in you as a result?* It's probably hard to think of an answer. When we

---

1. See *Struck Down but Not Destroyed: Living Faithfully with Anxiety* and *Finding Hope in Hard Things: A Positive Take on Suffering.*

receive a gift we like, we may have some gratitude, passing like a breeze over the hills. When we have success at work, we might be encouraged with a comment from someone else, or perhaps we gain a bit of confidence. But that, too, is fleeting. And if we enjoy the deep acceptance of another person, that's wonderful. But it may not change us very much. We enjoy it, and maybe we thank God for it, but it often ends there.

My point is this: We don't tend to change very much when we experience pleasant things. We stay the same. We're sail boats on a pond without any wind. We drift. And don't misunderstand me. It's okay to drift on the water sometimes. It's *good* to enjoy the blessings God sends our way. But the blessings we receive don't seem to have a history of pushing us to give to others.

Suffering and hardship, in my experience, have great shaping power. It's true that you can remain the same in suffering; you can even regress and become worse—more self-centered and tight-fisted and cold. But suffering also does what our blessings don't seem to do: reveal the passing nature of this life and call us to a deeper longing for communion with God that outlasts the pains of a punctured creation. Suffering calls us to give because it shows us what's worth giving: everything. We don't get to keep anything forever anyway.

If we can't hold on to anything here, if we're going to have to give up our very lives eventually, then why are we so fixated on holding as many blessings as we can carry, balancing a billion gifts in our arms as we stumble through the ordinary hours? You see, what keeps us from giving is often the illusion that we *can* hold on to everything we have. When we suffer, that illusion shatters like a glass on the kitchen floor. We realize with painful clarity that we can't keep everything, that we don't get to stay here forever, that it is more blessed to give than to receive because *giving* is what outlasts all else.

> *What keeps us from giving is often the illusion that we can hold on to everything we have.*

Many people have a very hard time with this truth. Biblically speaking, it's clear to me that we're called to live a suffering life because that was Christ's life, and we follow Christ. That's one of the many reasons why I've loved reading and practicing the lessons in Paul Miller's *J-Curve*.[2] Our moments and our days are not truly about growing in wealth and comfort. They're about growing through suffering, through little "deaths" each day in which we sacrifice ourselves (our ambition, our pride, our desires) so that others might experience the resurrection life of Jesus. That is the Christ-path before our feet each morning. We'd like to walk a different path, and many of us do, but that's not the path that Jesus walked. We are meant to suffer with him in order that we might be raised with him (Rom. 6:4;

---

2. Paul E. Miller, *J-Curve: Dying and Rising with Jesus in Everyday Life* (Wheaton, IL: Crossway, 2019). To see how this can apply to anxiety, see "Finding New Life in Your Anxiety," http://piercetaylorhibbs.com/finding-new-life-in-your-anxiety/.

Phil. 3:10).

Before you lose the smile on your face, remember that this is actually *good* news. The gospel is the good news of God. Why? Because none of us can walk the path of ease and comfort forever anyway. We're all going to experience hard things because we live in a broken world, filled with imperfect people. Maintaining the course of ease and comfort is an exercise in frustration. It's not going to happen. We're going to experience suffering. And if that's the case, isn't it good news to know that the God we serve not only loves us enough to suffer *with* us and *for* us; he also will use our hard things to make us more like himself? Isn't it encouraging to know that the hard things we face *always* have a brighter purpose than meets the eye?

Everyone else in the world can look at hard things—at anxiety disorders and cancer diagnoses and COVID pandemics—and try to flee. They run away. They avoid. They try with everything they have to evade suffering. And when they can't (and they *always* can't), they can easily turn bitter. But we run *toward* and *through* suffering with hope, because we know that God's up to something glorious. We feel the pain. We're not stoics. We weep with those who weep. And yet we don't grieve and lament in the same way that others do. We walk straight into suffering with our eyes fixed on Christ, who sympathizes with us in our suffering and calls us to die and rise with him.

I guess what I'm saying is just an echo what Paul Miller has already written, that the good news of the gospel isn't just *believing* in Christ, in what he's done to save us from sin and selfishness. It's also *becoming* like Christ. Many people want to believe, but they don't want to become. Suffering is what makes us become like Christ.

In short, there's a clear biblical relationship between suffering and giving. When we suffer, we become more like Christ, for we die and rise with him, and Christ is the self-giving God. Suffering is bound to make us givers because it's bound to make us more like Christ.

If you're interested in reading more about this on a personal level, check out *Finding Hope in Hard Things: A Positive Take on Suffering*. That's where I unpack how God has shaped me through my father's early death, my anxiety disorder, and my ongoing struggles with self-doubt. If you're suffering right now (and you probably are in some way), take heart. Christ has not only overcome the world (John 16:33); he's also promised to shape us as we walk through it, by the power of his own Spirit.

Appendix 2: Constant Givers Need Rest

My wife, to whom this book is dedicated, is one of the most giving people I know. It's like the eyes of her heart are always turned outward, scanning her surroundings for someone else's needs or wants. It's truly mind-boggling to me. I can't explain it, though I've been told that this is one of the gifts of motherhood. Still, even before she was a mother, she had this ability, this passion, this . . . gift.

And yet, one of the things I learned early on in our marriage and parenting is that constant givers need rest. You can't constantly give without meeting exhaustion. And when you meet exhaustion, you're *less* giving anyway. So, it's never good to get to that point.

What has this meant for me, and what might it mean for you? I used to think that it meant I needed to communicate constantly with my wife to see when she was feeling overwhelmed. And communication *is* critical, but then I realized that asking *her* to communicate her needs to me was another way of asking her to give herself. It wasn't a relief to her. I've been learning (and will learn for many years to come) the art of what I call *preemptive serving*. Preemptive serving is when you give a giver a break *before* she asks for it. You don't wait until that person communicates his or her exhaustion before you step in to give. Instead, you meet them on their path before they get there. They show up to do something, to give themselves again, and you say, "Actually, I've already taken care of that. Why don't you get some quiet time for a bit?"

This is *very* hard to do, especially when you're busy (but basically everyone could use busyness as an excuse, which means it's *not* really an excuse). When we fill our lives with tasks, when we're constantly in a hurry, there's no space to look to the needs of others. As John Mark Comer put it, "Both sin and busyness have the exact same effect—they cut off your connection to God, to other people, and even to your own soul."[1] Busyness will bleed you dry of your ability to give yourself to others, and that includes giving yourself to a constant giver. Consequently, you probably *can't* give a constant giver a break if you've taken on too much yourself. In the spirit of John the Baptist, it might be necessary for you to become smaller and simpler if you're going to serve Christ. You can't do everything. Or, as I like to tell my students, there's no addition without adaptation. If you want to serve a constant giver in your life, you're going to need to change how you do things. It's probably not going to work if you just try to pencil it in around your "more important" commitments. *This* is the more important commitment.

---

1. John Mark Comer, *The Ruthless Elimination of Hurry: How to Stay Emotionally Healthy and Spiritually Alive in the Chaos of the Modern World* (Colorado Springs, CO: Waterbrook, 2019), 20.

Practically speaking, one way to start is by communicating to a constant giver that you *see* him or her. You're aware of just how much giving is going on. And you want to relieve the pressure so that this giver can continue to be a giving light for Christ in a world that's running low on servants.

The next step is by doing a bit of personal research to find a way to give yourself to the giver. This does *not* mean that you ask him or her how you can provide some rest or relief. That always sounds like a good approach, and sometimes it's necessary, but asking someone else how you can help will often be translated into another task for the constant giver, something *else* to do, and that's if you can get the person to accept your offer in the first place (most will resist the help). Instead, you have to try to provide relief by studying the person's life and jumping ahead of him or her on the path. Here are some simple examples, some of which I've tried to do for my own wife.

- Making her coffee each morning before she asks
- Inviting her sister to plan an afternoon away from the kids, where they can just be sisters and not have to worry about serving others
- Working daily down time into the schedule each day (an hour or more if possible) so that your constant giver can get a break
- Talking with your constant giver about what he or she is up to so that you can find ways to help out before being asked

There are lots of ways to serve constant givers. The trouble is that constant givers are so giving that they start to feel *guilty* when they're not giving. You can help mitigate this if you step in front of a constant giver and offer rest. This is a way of saying, "Hey, it's okay for *you* to be served, for *you* to receive a gift. Really, it's okay."

The heart of giving, as the heart of God, is love. But when constant givers become overwhelmed and oppressed, guilt can replace love, and that can lead to soul injuries, both for themselves and those they serve.

My invitation is for you to find a constant giver in your life (for me, it's my wife) and start studying that person intently. How does this person give constantly? Where are there opportunities for service that would be appreciated? Where would this person *not* want you to give? Study the soul, and then plan your gifts.

Constant givers need rest. We all do, but they need it even more than the rest of us because they're always actively giving themselves away. And there's only so much self to give.

Feedback

I want to hear from you! Was this book helpful? Did it provide what you were hoping you'd find? Would you recommend it to a friend? The best way you can express your thoughts on the book and let others know about it is to leave a review on Amazon or Goodreads. This helps other strugglers get a sense of what they can expect from the book. It's also a huge help to writers! Would you do that for me? Just follow the instructions below for Amazon. It's similar for Goodreads.

- Go to my Amazon author page (amazon.com/author/piercetaylorhibbs) and click on this book.
- Click next to the Amazon rating, which will show you the current reviews.
- Click the button that says "Write a customer review."
- Follow the steps to leave your review.

I'm legitimately interested in what you think. Be honest. I promise I won't be offended. Thank you for reading the book! That in itself is a huge blessing to me.

Connect and Grow

Want to connect with me and grow in your spiritual development? You can join my email list to get free downloads that will help, and maybe you'll pick up some inspiration on the way. I'll keep you posted about new publications and give you exclusive content, too! There aren't any strings attached. To join, visit http://piercetaylorhibbs.com/subscribe-and-connect/. Right away, you get a free download of my ebook *In Divine Company: Growing Closer to the God Who Speaks.*

CPSIA information can be obtained
at www.ICGtesting.com
Printed in the USA
LVHW092124080421
683319LV00044B/592/J